Celebrate
with a Stitch

Mandy Shaw

D&C
BOURNEMOUTH

Contents

Foreword 4

Introduction 6

Get Ready to Stitch 8

BUNTING 22

NEW BABY 26
Baby Sampler 28
First Blanket 32
Dribble Bibs 34
Snuggle Rabbit 36
First Shoes 40
Baby Gift Bag 42

WEDDING 44
Wedding Bunting 46
Hanging Heart 48
Vintage Posies 50
Bridesmaids' Gifts 52
Ring Cushion 56
Top Table Lampshades 58

BIRTHDAYS 62
Birthday Cakes 64
Birthday Badges 68
Birthday Party Stitchery 70
Crowns and Tiaras 74
Seven More Sleeps 78

CHRISTMAS 86
Christmas Lampshades 88
Mini Tree Bunting 92
Christmas Pennant 96
Robin Decorations 98

CELEBRATION QUILT 100
Friendship Quilt 102

PENNANTS 104

Techniques 108

Templates 110

Acknowledgments, About
the Author and Suppliers 126

Index 127

Foreword

Mandy is a true creative – she fizzes with new ideas for designs and is buzzing with excitement about her latest book project. This collection of projects to celebrate everything from birthdays to babies, captures Mandy's contagious energy and enthusiasm as well as her unique style, making it a must for any crafter, new or experienced.

I first met Mandy when she showed me how to make a Christmas stocking using gorgeous vintage fabrics from my scrap stash. In this, her latest book, Mandy shows us how to make celebratory bunting, pennants and decorations using vintage and modern fabrics, that can be adapted for every occasion.

Immerse yourself in this fabulous selection of projects, which culminates with the ultimate 'Celebration Quilt' – an heirloom keepsake to be treasured forever.

Happy sewing!

Kirstie Allsopp

Introduction

When it comes to designing, making, creating and writing, my home and my family are always my inspiration, and why? Because we are always celebrating one event or another. Whether it's passing an exam, a birthday party, a family get-together, a birth or a marriage, Halloween or Christmas, it seems there is a celebration every month of the year.

Days spent together with friends and family make memories – the more we can cram in, the richer our lives will be. This book is about celebrating these occasions by the making of decorations and gifts.

No party is complete without bunting and I've got several different versions for you to make. My pennants are a quick fix for brightening up any event, and wine glass lampshades are perfect for decorating a party table. I have project ideas for celebrating the birth of a baby, a wedding celebration, a child's birthday party and Christmas – of course – but any of the ideas can easily be adapted to suit your own celebrations.

Get Ready to Stitch

If the great celebration ideas in this book and the beautiful photography have inspired you to get creative, but you are new to stitching, this chapter will give you all the advice you need to begin with confidence. There is helpful advice on choosing fabrics and threads, essential tips on working the appliqué designs, as well as hand embroidery stitch diagrams for both left- and right-handers. All the projects contain a variety of sewing techniques to teach you new skills and perhaps brush up on ones you already know.

Fabrics and Threads

The fabrics I have used for the projects in this book have a retro Fifties feel with lots of spots, checks and stripes. I used a colour palette of pastels and primary colours which, I hope you will agree, gives a fresh, bright look that will appeal to all ages.

FABRICS

If you are new to making things from fabric you are in for a great treat. You have so much to look forward to as you build your fabric collections, from sourcing fabric shops, to stashing your buys on little shelves or in a special drawer. I love to work with 100% cotton to give a clean, crisp textured look to my makes. It is advisable to wash and press your fabrics before you sew in case the colour runs. Fabrics are often treated with a sort of starch dressing to make them easier to sew; after washing and drying, you may find that giving your fabrics a little spray starch will aid sewing.

Felt

I adore working with felt as it does not fray; it is lovely to sew, and especially to blanket stitch. There are various qualities of felt, which perform differently with wear; always buy felt that has a percentage of wool in it – the higher the better – as this will help to prevent the felt's surface from going bobbly over time.

Vintage

Vintage fabrics are a favourite of mine – embroidered cloths, lace hankies, cotton monogrammed linens and similar treasures can be sourced from internet auctions, car boot sales and secondhand shops; you never know what you will discover.

Use a fabric spray adhesive to attach wadding (batting) to your fabric. Follow the manufacturer's instructions and spray the wadding (batting) not the fabric.

EMBROIDERY THREADS

As the projects call for different styles of stitching, I have used different types of embroidery thread. Stranded cotton (floss) is good for fine work but can be used to embroider thicker lines too, while coton à broder is sometimes too thick for the detailed work required on some projects, so mix and match as you choose.

Coton à broder

A favourite of mine, this single strand thread has a matt finish. It is available in different widths in several colours. I prefer No.16 which is quite thick and ideal for blanket stitching, outlining, backstitching, and quilting. Although shops rarely stock the whole range, they can be ordered.

Stranded cotton (floss)

This is available in skeins consisting of six strands which can be pulled out individually for use. It is most usual to use two strands in the needle, but for fine detail use just one, and for a chunkier stitching line use three or more.

Maderia Lana

This is a machine sewing thread that looks like wool and sews up a treat to give a hand blanket stitch appearance. You will need to use a larger size 16/100 needle; make sure you use a good-quality one as cheaper needles may have burrs that will shred the thread. For the bobbin thread, use an ordinary thread. Maderia Lana can also be used to hand quilt and embroider, and you will need to use a large-eyed, good-quality needle.

SEWING NOTIONS

When making up your projects, always use a good-quality sewing thread in a colour to match your chosen fabrics.

Invest in a pack of good-quality mixed embroidery needles. These have large eyes and are very sharp, piercing the fabric and allowing the thread to be pulled through with very little friction. How do you know what size needle to use? If after three attempts the needle won't thread, change to one with a larger hole. My personal favourites are sashiko needles size 12.

Working the Appliqué

Appliqué takes its name from the French verb *appliquer*, meaning to apply. The technique involves cutting fabric to shape and attaching it to a background fabric to create a surface decoration. The fabric shapes are held in position with fusible webbing and secured and embellished with hand or machine stitching.

WORKING WITH FUSIBLE WEBBING

Fusible webbing is an iron-on fabric adhesive that can be purchased in a roll or in pre-cut pieces and it looks like paper. One side is paper-backed and can be drawn on (so you can trace the motif you want) and the other has a thin membrane of glue that melts when heated by an iron to attach it to fabric. It is easy to use if you follow these simple step-by-step instructions.

1. Trace the motif you want onto the paper (smooth) side of the fusible webbing. Cut roughly around the drawn motif rather than following the drawn line accurately at this stage.

2. Iron the fusible webbing onto the wrong side of the appliqué fabric making sure that the fusible webbing is glue (rough) side down. The glue on the back of the fusible webbing melts when heated so be very careful to iron the paper side or else it will stick to your iron.

3. Once the fusible webbing has been attached to the appliqué fabric you can cut out the motif accurately on the drawn line.

4. Carefully peel off the backing paper and position the appliqué motif onto the fabric it is to be applied to. Iron to fix in place.

5. Always cover the edge of the appliqué with a stitch to seal the edges. This can either be done by hand or by machine.

Always remember, the smooth side of the iron goes to the smooth side of the webbing.

Many templates provided for the project appliqués are drawn in reverse (like the robin from the Christmas Pennant) so that they will be the right way round when you come to fuse and sew them.

Types of fusible webbing

There are several different types of fusible webbing on the market. Here is my guide to the brands you are most likely to encounter. Whichever you choose, always take the time to read the manufacturer's instructions before using.

Bondaweb. A fine brand that sews through really well, but in storage the fusible film has a tendency to peel off the paper, so only buy sufficient for each project. A hot steam iron is used to fix the adhesive.

HeatnBond Lite. The adhesive film on this product is a little thicker than Bondaweb, so it stores really well. It fixes with a silk setting and if you use a hot iron by mistake it will render the adhesive useless, so take care.

Lite Steam-a-Seam 2. This product has the ability to stick your appliqué in place temporarily until you are ready to iron it, so no pieces of appliqué will come flying off on your journey to the iron.

TIPS FOR HAND APPLIQUÉ

- Use sharp fine scissors to cut out your appliqué shapes to give you a clean cut edge to sew over.

- Always use an appropriate needle for your thread – my personal favourite is John James embroidery size 7– and adapt the size of your stitch to the scale of the appliqué motif.

- If you prefer to needle turned appliqué, add a 6mm (¼in) seam allowance to the pieces, and use a fine matching thread and needle.

TIPS FOR MACHINE APPLIQUÉ

- Use a new needle: for best results use a sharp denim variety size 90/14 or 80/12, although for fine appliqué use a finer 70/10.

- Reduce your top tension a little – no bobbin thread should show on the top. Practise on identical fabric and layers first.

- Use bobbin fill or cotton thread in the bobbin; if there is a hole in the bobbin case arm, thread your cotton through it to improve tension.

- Use the machine's needle-down facility to prevent stitches slipping.

- Use an open-toed embroidery/appliqué presser foot that has a cut-away on the underside to accommodate the raised appliqué.

- To start pull thread up to the top, sew a couple of stitches on top of each other, then cut the thread, to prevent threads tangling beneath.

- On curves, stop on the outside edge needle down, raise the presser foot and turn the fabric – stop and start as necessary.

If you overlap adjoining pieces of appliqué you will have only one edge to sew instead of two. For example, on the cupcake (Pennants) the case is tucked beneath the icing, so only the sides and the bottom edge of the cupcake case need to be sewn to secure it in place.

Before ironing the appliqué design in place, lay out the individual pieces to help you to establish the fusing order. For example, in the case of the birthday party table setting (Seven More Sleeps) the tablecloth is laid down first, then the cake is laid on top, and the braid for the cake band is added last.

It is not always necessary to stitch a fusible appliqué down, for example if the work is not going to be laundered or if it will not be subject to a lot of wear. A quick make decorative pennant, such as the 21st birthday pennant, does not always require the appliqué to be stitched in place.

Working the Stitches

It's amazing how a little embroidery can lift a design to make it even more interesting. I have included my favourite stitches here, with working instructions for both left- and right-handed sewers. If you are looking to refresh your embroidery skills, the Birthday Party Stitchery uses several of the stitches.

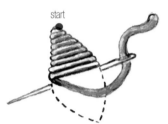

A filling stitch used to create a smooth surface decoration.

Transferring the embroidery designs

When transferring an embroidery design onto a cream background as for the Baby Sampler for example, you should be able to see through the fabric to trace off the design with a fine pencil. Alternatively, use a window as a 'light box' – tape the design to the window, tape your fabric on top and trace off using a pencil, fade away pen or other suitable marker.

Starting and finishing stitching

- Thread your needle – never use more than a short arm's length of thread at one time as it will be more prone to knotting, and more vulnerable to fraying and splitting.

- Start the embroideries with a small knot on the wrong side of the work. To avoid the knot being seen from the front of the work, do keep it small.

- When rejoining a thread, use your needle to weave the new thread into the previous stitches.

- When you have finished your embroidery, weave the thread into the previous sewn work.

- Do not leave long strands hanging on the back as these may show through on the front.

- It is a matter of personal preference as to whether or not you use an embroidery hoop to keep your fabric taut while stitching. I prefer not to as it gets in my way.

Right-handers

Work from right to left and take the stitches across from side to side, keeping them even and close; avoid stacking the stitches on top of each other or the effect will be unattractively lumpy. The stitches can be worked in a slanting direction or straight across the design.

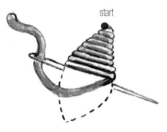

Left-handers

Work from left to right and take the stitches across from side to side, keeping them even and close; avoid stacking the stitches on top of each other or the effect will be unattractively lumpy. The stitches can be worked in a slanting direction or straight across the design.

RUNNING STITCH

Run the needle in and out of the fabric for a simple but versatile line stitch.

To work seed stitch sew running stitches at different angles.

Right-handers

Work from right to left. Bring the needle up through the fabric, make a stitch, and bring the needle down through the fabric again. Repeat, making sure the stitches and the spaces between the stitches are the same size.

Left-handers

Work from left to right. Bring the needle up through the fabric, make a stitch, and bring the needle down through the fabric again. Repeat, making sure the stitches and the spaces between the stitches are the same size.

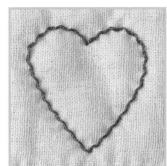

WHIPPED RUNNING STITCH

Whip a second thread through a line of running stitch for a decorative variation on this simple stitch.

Right-handers

Start by sewing the motif with a running stitch. For the best effect, keep the running stitches small. Working from right to left, pull the thread up from behind at the start point and slip the needle over and under one of the running stitches. Continue to whip the thread over in this way until all the running stitches are covered.

Left-handers

Start by sewing the motif with a running stitch. For the best effect, keep the running stitches small. Working from left to right, pull the thread up from behind at the start point and slip the needle over and under one of the running stitches. Continue to whip the thread over in this way until all the running stitches are covered.

BACKSTITCH

This is the perfect stitch when a well-defined outline is required.

This stitch may need a little practise to get neat and even. Uneven stitches will still give the desired effect.

Right-handers

Work from right to left. Begin by bringing the needle up a little ahead of where you want the line of stitching to start. Take the needle to the right, to the start position, back through the fabric to make a stitch, and bring it out to the left past the first stitch.

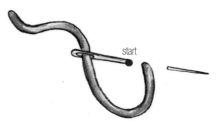

Each time a stitch is made, the thread passes back to fill the gap, for small stitches of an equal length.

Left-handers

Work from left to right. Begin by bringing the needle up a little ahead of where you want to start the stitching. Take the needle to the left, to the start position, back through the fabric to make a stitch, and bring it out to the right past the first stitch.

Each time a stitch is made, the thread passes back to fill the gap, for small stitches of an equal length.

BLANKET STITCH

This is a great border or edging stitch.

Aim to keep the length of the stitches even.

Right-handers

Work from left to right. Bring the needle up on the line of the motif or the edge of the appliqué. Take a stitch down from the line and bring the needle back where you started keeping the thread to the left.

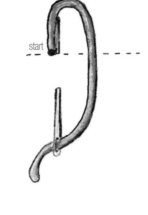

Insert the needle to the right of the first stitch, down from the line or edge, and bring it back out on the line or edge, making sure the thread is behind the needle. Pull through.

Continue repeating to make a line of stitches.

Left-handers

Work from right to left. Bring the needle up on the line of the motif or the edge of the appliqué. Take a stitch down from the line and bring the needle back where you started keeping the thread to the right.

Insert the needle to the left of the first stitch, down from the line or edge, and bring it back out on the line or edge, making sure the thread is behind the needle. Pull through.

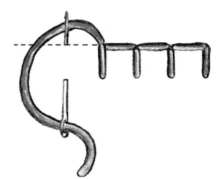

Continue repeating to make a line of stitches.

CHAIN STITCH

A series of looped stitches worked to interlink to form a chain-like pattern.

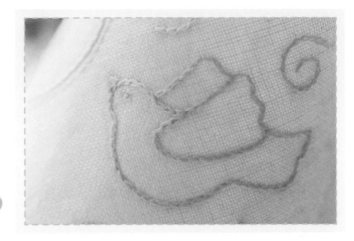

For a whipped chain stitch sew over the stitches again with the blunt end of the threaded needle.

Right-handers

Work from right to left. Bring the needle and thread up at the start point. Holding the thread to the left, put the needle back in where it first came out and bring the needle tip out again a little way beyond this point. Make sure the thread is under the needle and gently pull through.

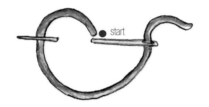

Put the needle in again beside the last stitch and continue. To secure the final stitch, sew a small straight stitch over the final loop.

Left-handers

Work from left to right. Bring the needle and thread up at the start point. Holding the thread to the right, put the needle back in where it first came out and bring the needle tip out again a little way beyond this point. Make sure the thread is under the needle and gently pull through.

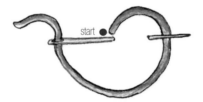

Put the needle in again beside the last stitch and continue. To secure the final stitch, sew a small straight stitch over the final loop.

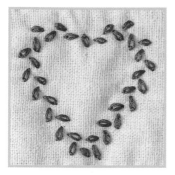

LAZY DAISY

A very pretty stitch related to the chain stitch.

If you pull the stitches tight you get long thin leaves or petals, if you sew them loosely they are plump and fat.

Right-handers

Work from left to right. Bring the needle up through the fabric at the top of the petal, hold the thread down with your thumb. Reinsert the needle at the start point and take it up again at the petal tip, keeping the thread under the needle.

Pull the thread through and, holding the petal down, make a little stitch at the tip to secure.

Left-handers

Work from right to left. Bring the needle up through the fabric at the top of the petal, hold the thread down with your thumb. Reinsert the needle at the start point and take it up again at the petal tip, keeping the thread under the needle.

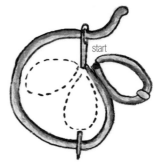

Pull the thread through and, holding the petal down, make a little stitch at the tip to secure.

HERRINGBONE STITCH

This stitch is a little tricky to get right, but it is well worth it as it always looks great even in small doses.

The motif line runs through the middle of the stitch.

Right-handers

Work from left to right. Bring the needle up below the motif line, cross over to the top right and take a little stitch to the left above the line.

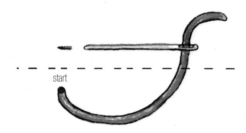

start

Cross over to the bottom right, and take a little stitch to the left. The needle should come out directly below the stitch above. Continue to line up the top end of a diagonal stitch with the bottom start of another for a nice, even line of stitching.

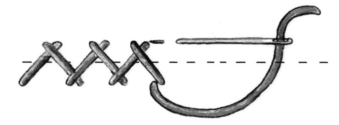

Left-handers

Work from right to left. Bring the needle up below the motif line, cross over to the top left and take a little stitch to the right above the line.

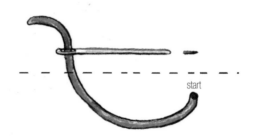

start

Cross over to the bottom left, and take a little stitch to the right. The needle should come out directly below the stitch above. Continue to line up the top end of a diagonal stitch with the bottom start of another for a nice, even line of stitching.

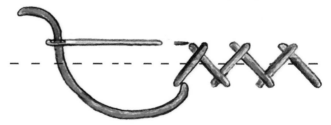

FRENCH KNOT

Embroidery experts may notice that my version of this is more often called a Colonial knot. It must be mastered.

For a larger or smaller knot wrap the thread around the needle more or less times.

Right-handers

Bring the needle up from the back of the fabric, and wrap the thread around the needle two or three times. Put the needle back into the fabric close to where it originally came out. Do not go back into the same hole otherwise the knot will be lost.

start

Before pulling the needle back through the fabric, gently pull up the thread that is twisted around the needle. Place your fingernail over the twist and pull through.

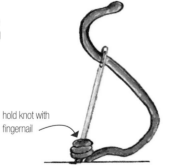

hold knot with fingernail

Left-handers

Bring the needle up from the back of the fabric, and wrap the thread around the needle two or three times. Put the needle back into the fabric close to where it originally came out. Do not go back into the same hole otherwise the knot will be lost.

start

Before pulling the needle back through the fabric, gently pull up the thread that is twisted around the needle. Place your fingernail over the twist and pull through.

hold knot with fingernail

CROSS STITCH

Most often seen worked in groups, discover the decorative power of the individual cross stitch.

Cross stitch can be used to create a star stitch when worked one on top of the other.

Right-handers

Work from left to right. Bring the needle up through the fabric. Take a stitch diagonally from the top left to the bottom right and bring the needle back out at the lower left corner.

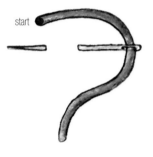

Take a stitch diagonally to the top right corner and bring the needle back where the next cross stitch is required. Pull the needle through to complete the cross stitch.

Left-handers

Work from right to left. Bring the needle up through the fabric. Take a stitch diagonally from the top right to the bottom left and bring the needle back out at the lower right corner.

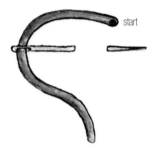

Take a stitch diagonally to the top left corner and bring the needle back out where the next cross stitch is required. Pull the needle through to complete the cross stitch.

STEM STITCH

An outline stitch with neatly overlapping lines.

Keep your stitches quite small as they do tend to grow in length.

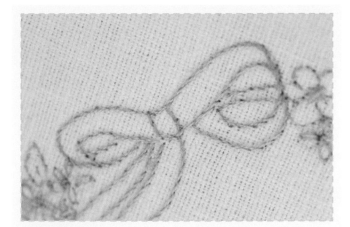

Right-handers

Work from left to right. Bring the needle up at the start point and make a stitch forward. Take a tiny stitch backwards from right to left. Pull the needle through, keeping the thread above the needle.

Take another small stitch to the right bringing the needle out near the hole of the last stitch.

As you continue to stitch the stitches take on a diagonal slant.

Left-handers

Work from right to left. Bring the needle up at the start point and make a stitch backward. Take a tiny stitch forwards from left to right. Pull the needle through, keeping the thread above the needle.

Take another small stitch to the left bringing the needle out near the hole of the last stitch.

As you continue to stitch the stitches take on a diagonal slant.

Bunting

There is nothing that says celebration quite like a string of bunting – just the sight of it fills me with joy. It invites you to come and have fun whatever the occasion. Hold a 'bunting bee': lay on the refreshments, borrow a few sewing machines and plenty of pairs of scissors, and invite family and friends to bring recycled fabrics to help you to make bunting for your party celebration.

To make standard bunting

1. Using the basic bunting template (see Templates), trace the flag outline onto paper, stick the paper onto cardboard and then cut out.

2. Using your cardboard template, cut out eight flags from the main fabrics, and eight flags from the lining fabric.

3. Cut out eight flags from the thin cotton wadding (batting), but make these 1.3cm (½in) larger all the way around.

The flags may have to be cut one the right way and the next upside down to make the most economical use of the fabric.

4. Cut eight pieces of wide ric-rac 46cm (18in) long. Sew the ric-rac to the right side of the main fabric flags, making sure the edge of the ric-rac lines up with the edge of the bunting. Do not sew along the top edge, and when you come to sew around the bottom of the flag, gently ease around the curve.

5. Turn the main fabric flag so that the wrong side is facing you and place it on top of a lining fabric flag, right sides together, then place on top of the cotton wadding (batting) so that it is lying in the middle of the wadding (batting). Pin well and sew all the way around, using the line of stitching you used to sew the ric-rac on as a guide, but do not sew along the top edge.

6. Trim your seams to a scant 6mm (¼in), even if this means you have to cut off some of the ric-rac.

7. Turn the flags the right way out and press well. Top stitch 6mm (¼in) in from the edge of the bunting either by hand or by machine.

8. Open out the binding and lay it right side to the flags, spacing the flags approx 5cm (2in) apart and leaving at least 25.5cm (10in) at the beginning and end of the binding flag-free for ties for hanging the bunting up. Sew the binding on with a 6mm (¼in) seam and press. Turn the binding over to the back of the flag and slip stitch in place. Turn under the ends of the bunting for a neat finish.

You will need for a length of standard bunting

- 30cm (12in) of 107cm (42in) wide main fabric in several coordinating colours
- 30cm (12in) of 107cm (42in) wide lining fabric
- 30cm (12in) of 107cm (42in) wide thin cotton wadding (batting)
- 4m (4⅜yd) wide ric-rac
- 2.25m (2½yd) of 1.3cm (½in) ready-made binding

Finished size: 2.25m (2½yd) length

To make vintage bunting

This bunting can be made to any length, and this is likely to depend on your what you can find to make it from. You will need to scour your cupboards, or your local second-hand shops. If you are lucky enough to find one large embroidered cloth you will be able to make at least a couple of metres/yards. Alternatively you can always make the bunting from lots of different linens.

Don't get sentimental about cutting up a piece of old embroidery: it's not use to anyone if it stays in the back of the cupboard for the rest of its life, so cut it up and use it to create some lovely new memories. Use the bunting card template and a pencil to mark out the flags onto your vintage embroidery finds – there is no need to worry about direction of the grain. Cut out as many flags as you can, trying to centralize the embroidery in the middle of the flag as much as you can. A chequered tablecloth makes a great lining fabric for the back of the flags.

To make baby bunting

Miniature bunting to decorate a baby's buggy is made in exactly the same way as the standard bunting, but omit the ric-rac edging trim and use the smallest bunting template (see Templates).

Pictured opposite, from top left clockwise:
- Baby bunting makes a great pram or cot decoration to welcome a newborn.
- A ric-rac trim gives your bunting that special touch.
- Vintage embroidered tray cloths are perfect for making bunting.
- There is no such thing as too much bunting.
- Adding extra embellishments such as small pearl buttons will make your bunting stand out from the rest.
- Different trims like these pom poms give a modern twist to your flags.

New Baby

I remember my granny saying: 'There's nothing like a new baby in the house.' Oh, how right she is! The overwhelming love you share for your new child – or grandchild – brings everyone closer.

Preparing for the baby is so exciting and gives you the perfect excuse to shop for some lovely fabrics to get creating. The things you make will become your family's future treasures.

The embroidered baby sampler would make a perfect christening present or newborn welcome card, and imagine the joy of receiving the snuggle rabbit as a gift. Make small fabric bags to wrap your baby presents, as I have for baby's first shoes. And if this is your very first attempt at gift-making, the first blanket, or one of the little bibs, is so very easy.

Baby Sampler

This sweet little embroidery, worked mainly in stem stitch, is a great way to decorate a nursery – simply change the colours of the embroidery thread and fabric frame to pink for a girl. Add baby's initial to the centre by scaling up the monogram alphabet (see Templates).

• •

1. Cut the light blue dot cotton fabric into three strips measuring 9cm (3½in) wide, then cut one of the strips in half. These are the sashing strips to frame the white linen fabric.

2. Pin one short sashing strip to one short edge of the linen fabric, right sides facing. Sew together with 6mm (¼in) seam allowance. Press the seam open and trim the sashing strip to match the linen fabric, if necessary. Join the second short sashing strip to the opposite edge of the linen fabric in the same way.

3. Now join the long sashing strips, one to either side, in the same way, again using a 6mm (¼in) seam allowance and trimming any excess fabric as necessary.

4. Trace the embroidery design (see Templates) centrally onto the white linen fabric.

5. Place the wadding (batting) behind the prepared work and tack (baste) in place (or lightly spray glue the two layers together).

6. Embroider the main design in stem stitch using two strands of stranded cotton (floss), and backstitch for the flowers.

7. Using one strand of stranded cotton (floss) and backstitch, embroider the baby's head, face and foot, add the details to the stork's beak and the fabric bundle ties, and embroider the heart onto the stork's wing. Again using just one strand of stranded cotton (floss) work French knots for the eyes and to make the flower centres to complete the embroidery.

You will need

- 16.5cm x 21.5cm (6½in x 8½in) white linen
- 33cm x 27cm (13in x 10½in) blue dot cotton fabric
- DMC stranded cotton (floss): blue 828
- 33cm x 28cm (13in x 11in) cotton wadding (batting)
- 30cm x 35.5cm (12in x 14in) felt
- 30cm x 35.5cm (12in x 14in) fusible webbing
- 30cm x 35.5cm (12in x 14in) medium-weight card
- 75.5cm (30in) white narrow ric-rac
- 80cm (32in) white wide ric-rac
- 15.5cm (6in) ribbon
- Small button

Finished size: 30cm x 35.5cm (12in x 14in)

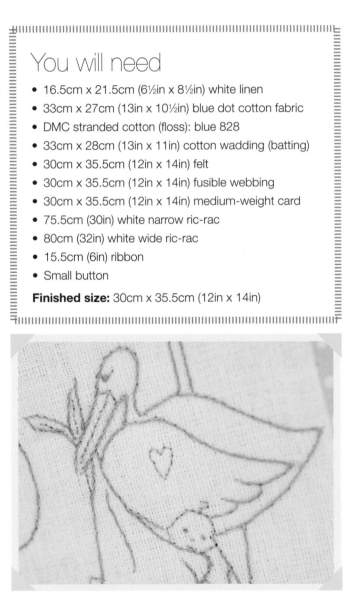

8. Starting in the bottom left-hand corner, sew the narrow ric-rac in place approx 6mm (¼in) from the inside edge of the light blue dot fabric frame. Sew the small button in place to cover the raw ends of the ric-rac braid.

Sew straight down the centre of the narrow ric-rac with matching thread. Ric-rac is very dense so using a finer sewing machine needle (size 12) will help.

9. Working on the wrong side of the stitchery, place the piece of card in the centre and fold over the fabric at the top, bottom and sides, securing in place with a few tacking (basting) stitches (Fig. 1).

10. Continuing to work on the wrong side, place the wide ric-rac so that only half-circles will be seen from the front. Tack (baste), and then sew in place all the way around the edge (Fig. 1).

11. To make a backing to neatly finish the sampler, prepare the felt backing with the fusible webbing and adhere it in place.

12. Fold the ribbon in half and sew the raw edges to the back of the sampler to make a hanging loop. The finished sampler is now ready to be hung.

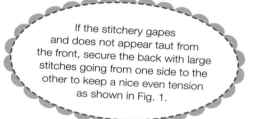

If the stitchery gapes and does not appear taut from the front, secure the back with large stitches going from one side to the other to keep a nice even tension as shown in Fig. 1.

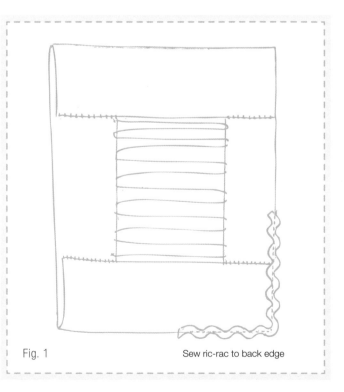

Fig. 1   Sew ric-rac to back edge

First Blanket

A newborn baby needs to be wrapped up in a light cotton blanket. This is the perfect design and it's so easy to make. Choose your fabric wisely, making sure it's soft and 100% cotton, but not too thick. I chose an adorable bunny print flannel for my top fabric and a blue stripe flannel for the backing.

....

1. Cut the front and backing fabrics square and place together with right sides facing. Using a suitable marker and a dinner plate, mark a curve at each corner and trim off. Pin well.

2. Sew all the way around the edge of the fabric, using a 6mm (¼in) seam allowance and leaving a 7.5cm (3in) gap on one side for turning.

3. Trim the seam allowance, especially around the corners, then turn the blanket the right way out. Press, then sew closed the opening

4. Use the embroidery thread to decorate all the way around the edge of the blanket with a large blanket stitch.

5. Working with fusible webbing (see Get Ready to Stitch), appliqué a long heart (see Templates) cut from contrasting fabric at each corner. Blanket stitch in place, sewing through both fabric layers.

6. To finish, embroider baby's initial in one of the appliqué hearts. Press, fold, wrap and give.

A fine fleece makes a good alternative backing fabric but will need pinning really well.

You will need...

- 1m (1yd) printed flannel
- 1m (1yd) striped flannel for backing
- 32cm x 32cm (12½in x 12½in) coordinating fabric for heart appliqué
- One skein of embroidery thread to match
- 25cm (10in) fusible webbing

Finished size: 97.5cm x 97.5cm (35in x 35in)

Dribble Bibs

This indispensable piece of baby clothing helps to keep baby's clothes clean for as long as possible. Essentially a bib, it doubles up as a decorative scarf/neckerchief. It is so easy to make that you could make several to match baby's favourite outfits.

1. Using the pattern supplied (see Templates) cut out two bib pieces, one from your chosen main fabric and one from the backing fabric: fold each piece of fabric in half, place the pattern on the fabric fold, then cut out.

2. Open out the cut fabric pieces and place together with right sides facing; pin well. Sew with a 6mm (¼in) seam leaving a gap for turning, as marked on the pattern.

3. Trim the seams to a scant 6mm (¼in). Turn the right way out and press to neaten. Top stitch all the way around the outside edge, encasing the opening.

4. To decorate the front of the bib, use a scrap of fabric to appliqué baby's initial and finish with a blanket stitch edging. Alternatively, you could embroider baby's name or an embroidery design (see First Shoes for how to embroider the little ducks design shown).

5. Sew one half of the popper to the top of one of the neck straps and the other half to the back of the other neck strap.

Dribble bibs make the perfect baby gift – make a trio, wrap in tissue and tie with a fancy ribbon.

You will need...

- 23cm x 30cm (9in x 12in) main fabric
- 23cm x 30cm (9in x 12in) flannel, fleece or thin towelling for backing
- Popper

Finished size: 20cm x 35.5cm (8in x 14in)

Snuggle Rabbit

As baby grows, there will be one toy that is favoured for snuggling up with at bedtime. There will be no rhyme or reason as to which, but if it can be one that has been handmade with love by you, so much the better. For this easy-to-make snuggle rabbit soft toy choose fabrics that have a soft finish; fine fleece, flannels or fine terry towelling are perfect.

1. Use the rabbit pattern (see Templates) to cut out the pieces required from your fabrics. First cut the body pieces: fold the fabric in half and half again, and place the pattern on the folds; cut one body from fleece and one from cotton fabric. From the remaining fleece cut the following pieces: head x 2, gusset A x 1, gusset B x 1, ears x 2. From the remaining cotton fabric cut two ears and two pocket pieces.

2. Place the pocket pieces right sides together and stitch all the way around leaving a gap at one side. Clip the corners, trim the curved seam, turn right way out and press. Top stitch along the top edge, then embroider the baby's initial on one side of the pocket (see Templates: Monogram Alphabet). Place the pocket onto the fleece body of the rabbit, initial side up, and stitch in place, first close to the edge, then 6mm (¼in) in from the edge.

3. Place the bodies right sides together; pin well and sew with a 6mm (¼in) seam allowance, leaving the gap at the neck as marked on the pattern. Place the heads right sides together and sew from A to B only.

4. Taking a cotton fabric ear piece and a fleece ear piece, place right sides together; pin and sew, leaving the bottom edge open as marked on the pattern. Repeat to make a second ear. Trim seams and turn the right way out. At the open end of the ears, with the cotton fabric facing up, fold in at either side to the middle and pin.

5. Pin the ears, cotton fabric side up, to the right side of gusset A (Fig. 1). Position the ears with a 6mm (¼in) seam allowance at either side for sewing the head together later.

You will need…

- 48cm x 48cm (19in x 19in) fleece
- 48cm x 48cm (19in x 19in) cotton fabric
- Polyester stuffing
- Sewing thread to match
- Blue embroidery thread

Finished size: 35.5cm x 25.5cm (14in x 10in) stretched out

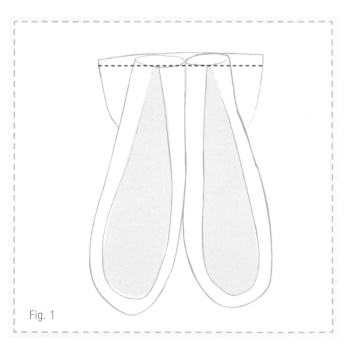

Fig. 1

6. Place gusset B over gusset A, right sides together and aligning the straight edges, and sew along this seam.

7. Pin the middle of the nose end of the gusset to the middle of the nose to neck seam A on the head; pin the other end to the back of the neck at C. Ease the rest of the head and gusset together and sew. Repeat to join the other side of the head, making sure you keep the ears well out of the way of any seam.

8. Gently stuff the head. Sew small gathering stitches around the neck edge, pull up tight and fasten off.

9. Embroider the rabbit's facial details with blue thread, working a cross stitch for each eye and a 'Y' for the nose (Fig. 2).

10. Open out the neck opening in the body and pin the head in place. Make sure the rabbit's head faces to the cotton fabric (front) side. Ladder stitch in place. Tie a single knot in each of the rabbit's paws. Keep your fingers crossed that your rabbit will be the chosen one.

Fig. 2

First Shoes

There is nothing sweeter than a pair of baby's feet adorned in these tiny slipper-shoes. Once grown out of, they will make a lovely hanging decoration for the nursery shelf. An ideal gift for a newborn, they can be embroidered in blue for a boy or pink for a girl. To hold the shape, place a scrunched up piece of coordinating fabric into each shoe when presenting as a gift.

1. Using the patterns supplied (see Templates), cut out two soles and two uppers from the white felt.

2. Transfer the embroidery design to the uppers using an iron-on transfer pencil (see Get Ready to Stitch), remembering to reverse the design for one of the shoes.

3. Following the photograph as your guide to the colours used, embroider the design using two strands of stranded cotton (floss). Use a backstitch for the ducks. The flowers are made by working two cross stitches on top of each other so that they make a star; work the flower stem with backstitch and use a lazy daisy for the leaves. Use blanket stitch to sew around the inner edges of the shoes. Using just one strand of the thread, stitch the little bees with tiny lazy daisy stitches to finish.

4. Working on one shoe at a time, match the pattern markings at the front and back of the sole and the upper to join and pin in place.

5. Overlap the back seam of each shoe by 6mm (¼in) and tack (baste) in place. Cut the ribbon in half and pin in place on each shoe to cover the back seam. Sew together with a 6mm (¼in) seam allowance working a backstitch by hand or by careful manoeuvring on your sewing machine.

6. Make a loop with the ribbon at the top of the back seam and finish off on the inside of the shoe by hand.

You will need...

- 25.5cm x 25.5cm (10in x 10in) white felt
- DMC stranded cotton (floss): yellow 0301, blue 828, pink 778, green 772
- 15.5cm (6in) of 5mm (¼in) wide ribbon

Finished size: 8cm x 5cm (3⅛in x 2in)

Baby Gift Bag

These little gift bags are easy to stitch and make a great alternative to traditional wrapping paper and ribbon. Once used for delivering your present, the bag can be used to store baby's treasured things.

● ●

1. Transfer the mother duck motif (see Templates: First Shoes) into the middle of the white felt square using an iron-on transfer pencil

2. Working with fusible webbing (see Get Ready to Stitch), appliqué the felt square onto the right side of one of the check fabric pieces, 10cm (4in) down from the top edge and centred. Blanket stitch in place using two strands of pink stranded cotton (floss).

3. Embroider the duck outline with backstitch and two strands of blue stranded cotton (floss).

4. Measure down 6.5cm (2½in) from the top of each piece of check fabric and make a 1.3cm (½in) cut at both of the sides. Fold in the side seams above where you have cut and press; stitch this seam to hold in place.

5. To form the casing to thread the ribbon through, fold over the top of each piece of check fabric by 4cm (1½in) to the wrong side and press. Turn under 6mm (¼in) on the raw edge and press. Stitch along the top of each side 6mm (¼in) from the folded edge, then stitch along the bottom turned under edge.

6. Place the two pieces of check fabric right sides together, and sew along the side and bottom seams with a 6mm (¼in) seam allowance. Carefully trim the corners and turn through to the right side.

7. Cut the ribbon in half. Pin a small safety pin to one end of the ribbon. Thread it through the left-hand side of the casing and all the way around to come out the same side as you started from. Tie the ends of the ribbon together with a small knot. Repeat for the other half of the ribbon but this time thread through from the right-hand side of the casing. When you pull the two sets of ribbon, the bag will close up beautifully.

You will need...

- Two pieces of check fabric each measuring 18cm x 20cm (7in x 8in)
- 4cm x 4cm (1½in x 1½in) white felt
- Fusible webbing
- 1m (40in) of 5mm (¼in) wide ribbon
- DMC stranded cotton (floss): blue 828, pink 778

Finished size: 16.5cm x 18cm (6½in x 7in)

Wedding

When it comes to the wedding ceremony, these days it seems anything goes. Couples are getting married abroad, on the beach, in castles, country houses, even tree houses – the list is endless. But for me, it is the simple homespun events that are the best.

There is nothing better than getting family and friends involved in the wedding preparations, from making invitations or a plate of food, to arranging the flowers or decorating the venue, for a truly memorable and personal occasion.

My wedding creations combine the old with the new. There are hanging hearts and wedding bunting made from vintage linens, and beautiful bridesmaids' gifts made from pearl buttons, as well as favour bags made from vintage serviettes. A dove motif embellishes a lovely appliqué ring cushion and an innovative embroidered wedding lampshade brings graceful elegance to the top table.

Wedding Bunting

No wedding is complete without bunting, and the making of it is a great way to get guests involved in the preparations. Organize a tea party and invite all the family, asking each to bring a piece of vintage textile. Give everyone a job – cutter, sewer, tea maker – and before you know it you will have lots of bunting made and ready to hang. The quantities given are for making a strand of eight flags – simply multiply to meet your requirements.

1. To make a pennant template, trace the wedding bunting pennant (see Templates) onto card and cut out. Use the card template to cut eight pennant flags from the calico, adding approx 2.5cm (1in) all the way around the outside of the pattern.

2. Choose a piece of vintage linen measuring approx 7.5cm (3in) square to go in the centre of each of the bunting pennant flags and pin in position. Place small pieces of lace and ribbon around and on top of the vintage linen square, stitching them down as you go and using them to cover any raw edges.

3. Once all the pennant flag fronts are decorated to your liking, press and spray starch the flags well.

4. Place a backing fabric square (this could be a piece of calico or a piece of vintage linen) on the back of the embellished pennant flag fronts, with wrong sides facing.

5. Take your card template and use a fine pencil or vanishing pen to mark out the pennant shape onto the right side of each fabric piece. Machine stitch on the marked line. Use pinking shears to cut out each pennant flag 6mm (¼in) away from the stitched line. Sew on a selection of buttons to the front of the flag pennants to complete the decoration.

6. Bind the top edge of the pennant flags (see Bunting) to complete the wedding bunting garland.

You could use the pennant flag bunting to decorate the top table, then make standard bunting (the traditional triangle shape using just one fabric layer) by the metre/yard to decorate the rest of the venue.

Hanging Heart

Hearts are synonymous with weddings and a whole bunch of hanging hearts made from vintage linens make great decorations. A single heart makes a great alternative to flowers for the bridesmaids to carry.

• •

1. Trace off the hanging heart pattern (see Templates) to make a card template and use this to mark out the heart shape onto one of the calico squares.

2. Choose a piece of vintage embroidered linen measuring approx 7.5cm (3in) square. Place this right side up in the middle of the heart and pin in place. Place small pieces of lace and ribbon around and on top of the vintage linen square, stitching them down as you go and using them to cover any raw edges.

3. Once the calico fabric has been decorated to your liking, cut out the heart shape (you may need to use your card template again as a guide). Sew on pearl buttons to complete the decoration.

4. Sew wide ric-rac to the right side of the decorated heart so that the humps are positioned on the raw edge of the fabric. Starting at the top of the heart, tack (baste) in place through the middle of the ric-rac.

5. Place the decorated heart onto the remaining calico square, right sides facing. Stitch the heart to the calico backing square along the ric-rac tacking (basting) line, leaving a gap along one side for stuffing.

6. Trim seams to a scant 6mm (¼in), snipping into the peak at the heart top and the point at the heart bottom. Turn the trimmed heart the right way out and stuff firmly with the polyester stuffing; carefully close the opening with ladder stitch.

7. Fold a 25cm (10in) piece of ribbon in half, turn under the raw edges and sew in place to the top of the heart with a button. Tie a bow from the remaining ribbon and stitch it to the heart just above the button.

You will need

- Two pieces of calico each measuring 20cm x 20cm (8in x 8in)
- Scraps of vintage lace, cotton and linen
- 1m (40in) of 1.3cm (½in) wide ribbon
- 1m (40in) wide ric-rac
- Polyester stuffing
- Pearl buttons

Finished size: 18cm x 20cm (7in x 8in)

Choose a plain fabric square to embroider the couple's initials or the date and time of the wedding. Take a photograph of it and use it as the wedding invite.

Vintage Posies

These simple little drawstring bags made from vintage serviettes are very easy to make. They can be filled with sugared almonds or a few dolly mixtures to make sweet favours for the wedding guests. Look for pieces that have some embroidered decoration on the corners in colours to match the wedding scheme. Thick linen serviettes are not suitable for this project, but fine small hankies will make lovely delicate posies.

1. Launder and spray starch the serviettes/napkins. Iron all four corners into the middle so that the corners are nearly touching (Fig .1).

2. Working 1.3cm (½in) in from the folded edge of the square, sew all the way around either by machine or by hand using a small running stitch (Fig. 1). This makes a casing to thread the ribbon through.

3. Cut the ribbon in half. Take one of the ribbon lengths and pin a small safety pin to one end to act as a threader. Starting at the bottom left-hand corner, thread the safety pin through the casing and ease it all the way around to come out again where you started. Do not pull up the ribbon yet, but do unpin the safety pin and tie the ribbon ends together in a loose knot.

4. Starting at the opposite (top right-hand) corner, thread the second piece of ribbon through the casing in the same way.

5. Fold over the pointed corners of the square to the wrong side and catch each down with a stitch.

6. Taking the ribbons in either hand, pull up tightly and tweak the four flaps to create the desired effect.

7. Untie the knots at the ends of the drawstring ribbons to thread on a decorative bead, then re-tie the knots securely.

8. Loosen the drawstring ribbons to fill the completed posies with sweets or treats.

Choose beads with holes big enough to thread the narrow ribbon through.

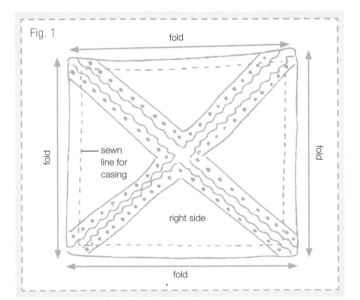

Fig. 1

fold

fold

fold

fold

sewn line for casing

right side

Bridesmaids' Gifts

It is a tradition to give the bridesmaids a thank you gift and these little pieces of jewellery – an easy-thread bracelet and a heart-shaped brooch – made from pearly buttons are ideal. They would also make perfect mementoes for those VIP wedding guests – the mother-of-the-bride and the groom's mother. Present them beautifully gift wrapped in a vintage posy.

To make the button brooch

1. Using the template supplied (see Templates), cut three hearts from the felt. Set one heart aside.

2. Place the other two hearts together and blanket stitch all the way around the edge using the cream embroidery thread to give you a double-layer heart.

3. Sew the buttons onto the double-layer heart. First sew the buttons on in a single layer around the outside edge, and then fill in the middle. There is no need to fasten off each button – simply take the needle right through to the back of the heart and skip across. Sew the remaining buttons on top of the first layer filling in any holes.

4. To finish the back neatly, sew on the set-aside heart using blanket stitch. Securely stitch the brooch clasp to the back of the button brooch.

You could use a piece of recycled wool blanket instead of the felt.

You will need for the button brooch

- Approx 40 small pearl buttons
- 23cm x 23cm (9in x 9in) cream felt
- Cream embroidery thread
- Large brooch clasp

Finished size: 6cm x 6cm (2⅜in x 2⅜in)

You will need for the button bracelet

- 1m (40in) of medium cotton thong
- 11 medium four-holed buttons

Finished size: approx 20cm (8in) long but can be adjusted to fit wrist size

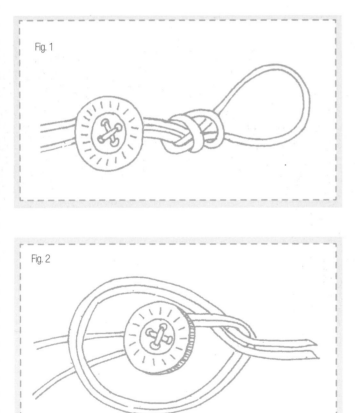

Fig. 1

Fig. 2

To make the button bracelet

1. Start by preparing the cut ends of the cotton thong by dipping them in a little heated candle wax, to prevent them from unravelling.

2. Fold the cotton thong in half, and at the end where the loop is, make the starting knot (Fig. 1). Make sure that the loop of the knot is big enough for you to pass one of your buttons through as this is the bracelet fastener: it should be neither too big nor too small, but just the right size.

3. Thread the thong ends into the back of the first button using two holes that are side by side. Thread the button right up to the knot. Take one thong end and place it into the hole diagonally opposite it; repeat with the other thong end (this is just like sewing a cross stitch). Pull tightly.

4. Take a second button and repeat step 3, threading the button right up tight to the previous one (note, the thongs at the back of the buttons should be parallel to each other). Continue threading on buttons in the same way until the bracelet fits snugly around the wrist (note, the exact number of buttons required will vary according to the size of the wrist). Don't worry if the bracelet seems to twist a bit; it will lay flat once worn.

5. To finish off the bracelet, wrap the thong ends around the final button at least once, and twice if possible, and pull tightly (Fig. 2). Cut the ends off 6mm (¼in) away from the button.

If you prefer you could make your bracelet using small (approx 17) or large (approx eight) buttons, but do not be tempted to mix the sizes.

Ring Cushion

It is all the little details that give an individual and personal feel to the wedding day, especially the homemade ones. This cutwork cushion is perfect for the presentation of the wedding rings during the marriage ceremony. Afterwards it can be used as a bedroom accessory to remind the happy couple of their perfect day.

1. Trace two doves (body and wing, one in reverse) and the full heart design (see Templates) onto the fusible webbing and roughly cut out around the outside edge of the marked outlines. Iron the fusible webbing pieces onto the cream felt. Thick felt may need to be ironed from both sides to successfully adhere the fusible webbing. Take care not to scold the fabric.

2. Carefully cut out the heart design and doves from the felt using small scissors (this will be a challenge depending on how thick your felt is). The neater the cut, the easier it will be to blanket stitch the appliqué later. Fuse the cut-out felt heart so that it is centred on one of the linen squares. Referring to the photograph, fuse the doves in the heart.

3. Transfer the bride and groom monograms (see Templates: Monogram Alphabet) onto the linen towards the bottom of the heart, and embroider using chain stitch and coton à broder thread.

4. Blanket stitch the felt appliqué in place by hand or machine using cream thread.

5. Tie the silk ribbon in a bow in its centre and sew the bow above the doves' heads. Sew the ribbon tails securely to the doves' beaks at either side leaving the ends loose for tying on the rings.

6. Starting down one side of the decorated cushion front, right side facing, pin the ric-rac braid along the edges, aligning the edge of the ric-rac with the raw edge of the fabric and gently curving the ric-rac around the corners. Tack (baste) the ric-rac in place 6mm (¼in) from the edge, sewing down the middle of the ric-rac so only little half moons show on the finished cushion (see Techniques).

You will need

- Two pieces of white linen each measuring 25.5cm x 25.5cm (10in x 10in)
- 20cm x 20cm (8in x 8in) cream felt
- 20cm x 20cm (8in x 8in) fusible webbing
- Polyester stuffing
- DMC coton à broder: cream 3033
- 105cm (42in) cream wide ric-rac
- 50cm (20in) narrow silk ribbon

Finished size: 25.5cm x 25.5cm (10in x 10in)

7. Take the second linen square and pin the cushion front to it with right sides together. Using the ric-rac tacking (basting) line as your guide, sew around the edges, leaving a small gap in one side. Trim seams and corners. Turn the cushion right way out, stuff, then sew the gap closed.

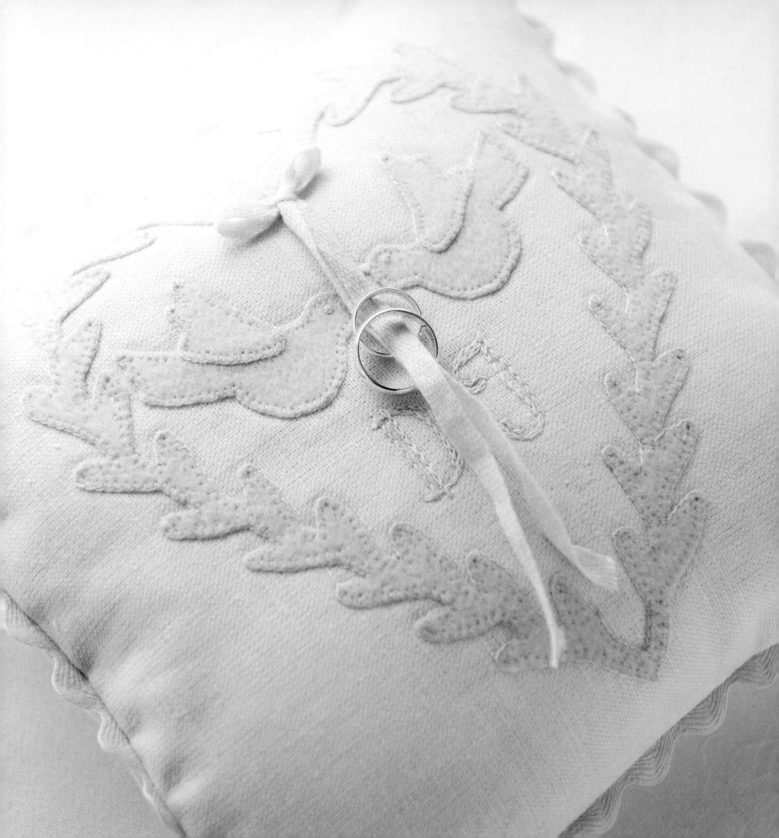

Top Table Lampshades

These wine glass lampshades are the sweetest way to decorate a celebration table. They are designed to button around a bowl-shape glass – a large white wine glass is the best – that has a battery night light placed inside it. They are a great way to make the bridal party's table look extra special. I have embroidered my design onto linen fabric, although as an alternative these could simply be made from vintage embroidered linens.

....

1. Using the lampshade template supplied (see Templates), trace off the outline onto a folded piece of paper as marked and cut out. Open up the paper pattern and glue it onto thin card to give you your full lampshade template.

2. Mark around the template onto thick iron-on interfacing; cut out and set aside. Place the template in the middle of the linen fabric and draw around it using a pencil.

You will need

- 35cm x 20cm (14in x 8in) linen type fabric
- 30cm x 20cm (12in x 8in) thick iron-on interfacing
- 30cm x 20cm (12in x 8in) lightweight iron-on interfacing
- Cream stranded cotton (floss)
- Five small pearl buttons
- 1m (40in) of 2cm (¾in) ready-made binding tape

Finished size: 33cm x 10cm (13in x 4in)

3. Transfer the embroidery design (see Templates) onto the front of the fabric, and then iron the lightweight interfacing onto the wrong side of the fabric, centring it over the embroidered design.

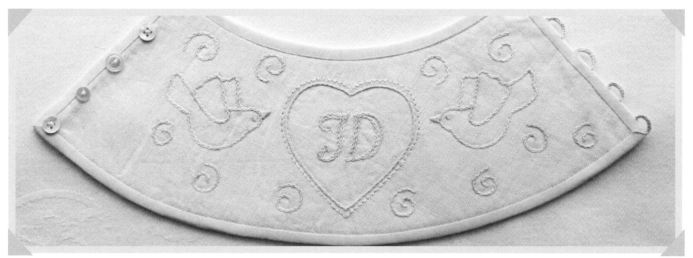

4. Stitch the embroidery design using two strands of thread throughout. Embroider the heart, the birds and the swirls with chain stitch, and use a large French knot for the birds' eyes and satin stitch for their noses. Whip the chain stitch around the heart and sew a row of backstitch around the edge to outline it. Embroider the couple's initials in the centre of heart (see Templates: Monogram Alphabet).

5. Once you have finished the embroidery, press the fabric well. Iron or spray glue the thick interfacing onto the wrong side of your work, making sure the embroidery design is centralized in it. Trim the linen fabric to the size of the interfacing.

6. Bind around the outside edge of the lampshade using ready-made binding tape starting at one of the top corners and mitring the other corners (see Techniques: Using ready-made binding).

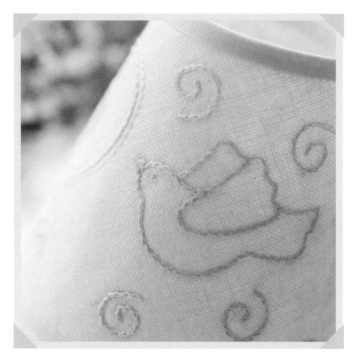

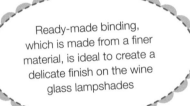

Ready-made binding, which is made from a finer material, is ideal to create a delicate finish on the wine glass lampshades

7. Mark on the button positions along one side of the lampshade and make the bar tacks on the opposite side (see Techniques: Making bar tacks). Finally, sew the five pearl buttons in place.

When using vintage embroidery to make your shade, choose the best part of the embroidery to show in the centre of the shade. Cutwork motifs work especially well for the table top lampshades.

Birthdays

There are six of us in my house and with the extended family added, we have at least one birthday a month – that's a lot of celebrating. Birthdays are a good excuse to bake, decorate and invite friends over to party.

I have a whole cupboard dedicated to making birthday cakes and decorating them, and a drawer full of candles, serviettes, party poppers and paper chains, and that's not even mentioning the shelf full of bunting. Childhood whizzes by so fast so fill it with lovely memories that your children will take forward into the future to share with children of their own.

This chapter is full of projects to make a child's birthday very special, from a wall hanging that counts down the sleeps until the birthday boy or girl's special day, to a party crown and tiara. A birthday stitchery celebrates a traditional birthday tea party and a fabric birthday cake makes a stunning centrepiece whatever your age, whether you be six or 60 plus!

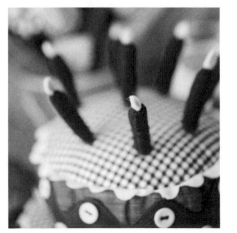  

Birthday Cakes

I have made each of my four children a themed cake to celebrate every one of their birthdays, and, as my eldest is now 27 years old, you could say that I am quite an expert on cake design. From treasure chests to trains, clowns to teddy bears, none of my cake designs has given me quite as much pleasure as these fabric ones, which make great portable decorations for a birthday outing. The you will need list gives the fabric requirements for the red check/spot cake, but you can easily change the fabrics to suit the birthday boy or girl.

To make the bottom layer

1. Using a 20cm (8in) dinner plate as a template cut out two circles from fabric 1 and two from the wadding (batting). Cut a 9cm x 63.5cm (3½in x 25in) strip from the wadding (batting) to match the fabric 2 strip. Spray glue, or tack (baste) if you prefer, your fabric pieces to the wadding (batting) pieces.

2. Decorate the centre of the strip with decorative tape. (Alternatively, you can use strip of fabrics 2 or 3 as I have done; there is no need to hem this if you use ric-rac braid to further decorate its edges.) To represent the cake's icing, tack (baste) ric-rac along the top and bottom edges of the fabric strip, attaching it to the right side so the raw edges align (see Techniques) and sewing in place along the tacking (basting line). Join together the two short ends of the decorated fabric strip to form a circle and sew with a 6mm (¼in) seam allowance.

3. Fold each circle in half and half again and finger press; open out and mark quarter folds with a pin around the edges. To find the matching quarters of the joined strip, lay it flat on your work surface, fold it in half and finger press; open it out again and mark each quarter with a pin.

4. Match up the pins on the circular strip to the pins on the circles, joining the pieces with right sides facing; pin and tack (baste), then sew together with a 6mm (¼in) seam allowance.

5. Carefully cut a slit in the middle of the top circle and turn it through to the right side. Stuff the cake very firmly with polyester stuffing, then ladder stitch the slit together. (This will be hidden when the top layer of the cake is added.)

To make the top layer

1. Using a 15.5cm (6in) tea plate as a template cut out two circles from fabric 1 and two from the wadding (batting). Cut a 6.5cm x 48.5cm (2½in x 19in) strip from the wadding (batting) to match the fabric 3 strip. Spray glue, or tack (baste) if you prefer, the fabric pieces to the wadding (batting) pieces.

2. Cut the hook-and-loop fastener into eight 5mm (³⁄₁₆in) squares, and separate the hooks from the loops. Working on the right side of one of the fabric circles, arrange the hook squares in a circle, with one in the middle, and sew in place. Set aside the loop squares to attach to the bottom of the fabric 'candles' later.

3. Make the top layer of the cake in exactly the same way as the bottom layer, except this time sew the ric-rac in the top seam only and cut the turning/stuffing slit on the base of the cake, that is the side that does *not* have the hook-and-loop fastener tape attached.

4. Place the top layer of cake on top of the bottom layer so that it is centred to cover the ladder stitch seams. Join the two cake layers together with ladder stitch (see Techniques: Utility stitches) using a strong, doubled thread. You may need to sew round the cake twice.

To make the candles

1. Cut pieces of felt 5cm x 10cm (2in x 4in). Starting at one short edge, roll up each piece of felt into a tube and stitch to hold in place.

2. Cut out a yellow felt 'flame' for each candle and fold in half. Tuck a flame into the middle of the candle and secure with a stitch. Sew the loop squares to the bottom of the candles. All that remains is to attach the candles onto the top of the cake by matching up the hook-and-loop squares.

Hook-and-loop fastener coins are available and these make for a neater finish when attaching the candles to the top layer of the cake.

You can further decorate the cake sides by pinning on a number birthday badge to suit the age of the birthday boy or girl.

Birthday Badges

I have used these simple-to-make rosette-style badges to decorate the front of my fabric birthday cakes, but they could just as easily be given instead of a card. Just appliqué on a number to let the world know just how old the party boy or girl is. They are ideal for those all important big birthdays too, from 1 to 100!

1. Trace off the birthday badge oval (see Templates) onto paper, glue it to lightweight card and cut out to make a template. Use the template to mark the oval onto the cardboard and cut out on the line. Cut a piece of wadding (batting) the same size and glue onto the cardboard oval.

2. Cut out a piece of background fabric 2.5cm (1in) bigger than the oval template all around. Appliqué a number centrally onto the fabric followingn the instructions for working with fusible webbing (see Get Ready to Stitch), and hand or machine blanket stitch in place.

3. Work a row of running stitches 6mm (¼in) in from the raw edge of the background fabric oval, starting your stitching with a knot and working the first three stitches on top of each other. When you return to your start point, do not cast off.

4. Place the wadding (batting) side of the cardboard oval to the wrong side of the background fabric oval, pull up your gathering stitches tight around the cardboard and cast off thoroughly.

5. To add a ribbon or lace trim rosette-style, work a line of gathering stitches close to the edge along one long side of the ribbon or lace and pull up the gathers to fit around the outside edge of your oval; join the raw ends and cast off your gathers. Glue or sew the frill to the wrong side of the oval close to the edge so that the frill will show on the right side. Alternatively, attach your chosen trim all the way around the outside edge of the oval.

You will need

- 7.5cm x 10cm (3in x 4in) background fabric
- 5cm x 7.5cm (2in x 3in) fabric for number appliqué
- 7.5cm x 10cm (3in x 4in) wadding (batting)
- 5cm x 7.5cm (2in x 3in) fusible webbing
- 6.5cm x 9cm (2½in x 3½in) felt
- Ribbon, ric-rac or pom-pom trim
- 6.5cm x 9cm (2½in x 3½in) cardboard
- Brooch pin

Finished size: 6.5cm x 9cm (2½in x 3½in)

6. Use the oval template to cut a backing piece from the felt. Glue or sew the felt oval onto the back to cover card and edges of the trim. Sew on the brooch pin 2.5cm (1in) from the top of the badge.

With so many birthdays to celebrate each year, it makes sense to make and keep a birthday badge card template alongside your stash of birthday cards.

Birthday Party Stitchery

This lovely stitchery is reminiscent of a birthday party scene straight out of an Enid Blyton story. It makes for a very special decoration to be hung up in your home to mark each birthday celebration. As only a few stitches are used – backstitch, running stitch, cross stitch and the odd French knot – it is a great starter piece.

Use a light box to aid the transfer of the embroidery design onto the linen, or tape the design, then the linen, to a window for a better view.

You will need

- 25.5cm x 25.5cm (10in x 10in) linen fabric
- DMC stranded cotton (floss): red 0047, brown 0375, blue 0142, light blue 0140, green 0242, dark pink 0039, flesh 0276, yellow 0301
- 25.5cm x 25.5cm (10in x 10in) lightweight fusible interfacing
- 20cm x 20cm (8in x 8in) red felt
- 20cm (8in) of 2.5cm (1in) wide pre-gathered ribbon
- Small piece of narrow ribbon for hanging
- 18cm (7in) diameter wooden embroidery hoop
- 25.5cm x 25.5cm (10in x 10in) card
- Strong fabric glue

Finished size: approx 18cm (7in) diameter

1. Carefully trace the embroidery design (see Templates) onto the front of the linen fabric using a fine pencil. Iron the interfacing onto the back of the fabric.

2. Embroider the design working backstitch using two strands of thread for the outlines and filling in the details as advised – see Embroider the Design.

3. Once the embroidery design has been completed, it may require a light hand wash. Leave to dry, then press.

4. Make a decorative backing for the birthday stitchery. Use your wooden hoop as a guide to draw a circle onto the card and cut out. Glue the red felt to the card and trim neatly to the edge of the card. With the card side facing up, glue the pre-gathered ribbon to the inner edge of the card, and set aside to dry.

5. Separate the embroidery hoop into its two parts. Place the embroidery over the smaller hoop, making sure you centralize the design. Place the larger hoop over the fabric and push it onto the smaller hoop. Pull the fabric taut and tighten the tension screw.

6. Working at the back of the hoop, trim the excess fabric to approx 5cm (2in). Using thread doubled in the needle and secured with a large knot, sew a running stitch 6mm (¼in) from the edge of the fabric, gather up tightly and fasten off.

7. Apply glue all around the edge of the back of the framed embroidery and stick it down onto the backing, card side facing up. Leave to dry, then fold the small ribbon length in half and glue it to the back of the embroidery so it can be hung up with pride.

Embroider the design

Brown (DMC 0375)

Using two strands: backstitch the outline edge of the chairs and the dog, and the hair outlines of the boy and centre girl.

Using one strand: backstitch highlights in the boy's and girl's hair; embroider small running stitches to fill the chair outlines; sew small tiny stitches (seed stitch) randomly all over the dog.

Work a French knot for the dog's eye and satin stitch for his nose. Work straight stitch detailing for the party guests' eyes and eyebrows.

Red (DMC 0047)

Using two strands: backstitch the bunting string and the outline of two of the flags. Decorate the flags with cross stitch. Continuing with backstitch, outline the outer and inner border of the large pennant, the dog's neckerchief, and the tablecloth decoration. Decorate the crowns with star stitch (made by working two cross stitches one on top of the other, at different angles).

Using one strand: work a French knot for the cherry on top of the cup cake; sew tiny running stitches to the pennant border, backstitch the stripes on the boy's t-shirt, the circles on the dog's neckerchief, and the inner border of the girl's rosette (you can add an age inside too).

Blue (DMC 0142)

Using two strands: backstitch the three crowns, the tablecloth, the outline of two of the bunting flags, one of the balloons and the centre girl's top.

Using one strand: seed stitch the blue balloon, decorate the two bunting flags with tiny squares, and chain stitch the candles.

Light blue (DMC 0140)

Using two strands: backstitch the outline of the boy's t-shirt.

Green (DMC 0242)

Using two strands: backstitch the outline of two of the bunting flags, one of the balloons, and the hanging string of the pennant, and the shoes of the left-hand girl.

Using one strand: seed stitch the balloon, decorate the flags with tiny squares, outline the birthday card with backstitch, add the lines of cross stitch and backstitch on the cake tiers, and the ribbon edging on the centre girl's rosette.

Dark pink (DMC 0039)

Using two strands: backstitch the outline of the left-hand girl's dress, one of the balloons, and the birthday cake.

Using one strand: seed stitch the balloon and work lines of running stitch for the sleeve detailing and waistband on the left-hand girl's dress.

Flesh (DMC 0276)

Using two strands: backstitch the outlines of the arms, legs and faces of the party guests.

Yellow (DMC 0301)

Using two strands: backstitch the details of the left-hand girl's hair, the birthday card, the socks of the left-hand girl, the outline of one of the bunting flags and the appropriate age number in the pennant.

Using one strand: embroider a single chain stitch for the flame on top of each of the candles.

Take a photograph of your finished stitchery and use to make your very own birthday cards.

Crowns and Tiaras

These impressive party hats will make the birthday boy or girl feel really special. There is a pretty pink tiara for the Queen for the day and a bold crown for the King for the day. Made to fit children, the size is easy to adapt for adults too.

To make the tiara

1. Trace the full tiara pattern (see Templates) onto the fusible webbing. Fuse the webbing to the felt and cut out, making sure you also cut out the heart shapes.

2. Peel off the backing paper from the fusible webbing. Cut two squares of pink check fabric large enough to cover the small cut-out hearts and place on the fusible webbing side of the tiara. Do not iron in place, but pin from the right side of the tiara. Cut a piece of vintage embroidery to cover the large heart in the same way.

3. Lay the tiara wrong side down onto the thick interfacing and iron in place. Place a cloth over the tiara while you iron so you do not scold the felt. Press firmly until the interfacing has fused. Trim the interfacing to the tiara's shape.

4. To decorate the tiara, sew the decorative tape along the bottom edge, then sew the narrow ric-rac along the top edge of the tape and continue around the top edge to outline the tiara's shape. Hand-stitch a running stitch border around the outer edge of the hearts using pink embroidery thread. Sew on the small pearl buttons using the photograph as a guide

5. Finally attach the elastic to the side edges of the tiara, adjusting the length to fit the birthday girl's head.

You will need for the tiara

- 15.5cm x 46cm (6in x 18in) pink felt
- 10cm x 14cm (4in x 5½in) pink check fabric
- 23cm x 20cm (9in x 8in) vintage embroidery
- 15.5cm x 46cm (6in x 18in) fusible webbing
- 15.5cm x 46cm (6in x 18in) thick interfacing
- 43cm (17in) of 1.3cm (½in) wide decorative tape
- 86cm (34in) narrow ric-rac
- Nine pearl buttons
- 20cm (8in) of 2.5cm (1in) wide elastic
- Pink embroidery thread

Finished size: 42cm x 13cm (16½in x 5in)

You will need for the crown

- 15.5cm x 46cm (6in x 18in) denim
- 15.5cm x 46cm (6in x 18in) fusible webbing
- 15.5cm x 46cm (6in x 18in) thick interfacing
- 6.5cm x 6.5cm (2½in x 2½in) yellow felt
- 43cm (17in) of 1.3cm (½in) wide decorative tape
- One large and two small red buttons
- 20cm (8in) of 2.5cm (1in) wide elastic
- Three pom poms
- Red sewing thread

Finished size: 42cm x 13cm (16½in x 5in)

To make the crown

1. Trace the full crown pattern (see Templates) onto the fusible webbing. Fuse the webbing to the denim and cut out, making sure you also cut out the diamond shape.

2. Peel off the backing paper from the fusible webbing. Use the yellow felt to cover the cut-out diamond and place on the fusible webbing side of the crown. Do not iron in place, but pin from the right side of the crown.

3. Lay the crown wrong side down onto the thick interfacing and iron in place. Press firmly until the interfacing has fused. Trim the interfacing to the crown's shape.

4. To decorate the crown, sew the decorative tape along the bottom edge. Using red thread, machine stitch around the outside edge of the crown and to create a border around the diamond.

5. Sew the large red button in the middle of the diamond and the two small buttons on either side of the diamond. Glue the pom poms to the tips of the points of the crown.

6. Finally attach the elastic to the side edges of the crown, adjusting the length to fit the birthday boy's head.

Seven More Sleeps

This sweet little house-shaped wall hanging is the ideal way to help small children anticipate their big day. Bertie the bear moves bed every night to count down how many more sleeps there are to go, then on the day itself the double doors at the base of the hanging are opened to reveal a traditional birthday party scene which Bertie can be poppered into.

Note: It is important when making the wall hanging to cut and sew very accurately to ensure it fits together well. Use a rotary cutter, mat and ruler if you have them. Use 6mm (¼in) seams throughout: to keep your seams accurate, use a quarter-inch foot on your sewing machine if possible. All measurements given have had seam allowances added. Lightly spray starch all your fabrics before starting work to make the folding nice and sharp.

You will need

- 50cm (20in) of 107cm (42in) wide denim for the background
- 25.5cm (10in) of 107cm (42in) white cotton for the bed sheets
- 60cm x 84.5cm (24in x 33in) printed fabric for the lining
- Seven pieces of assorted printed fabrics each measuring 11.5cm x 6.5cm (4½in x 2½in) for the bedspreads
- 48.5cm x 16.5cm (19in x 6½in) green striped fabric for the birthday party scene
- 60cm x 84.5cm (24in x 33in) cotton mix wadding (batting)
- 46cm x 23cm (18in x 9in) fusible webbing
- 25.5cm x 15.5cm (10in x 6in) thick interfacing
- 15.5cm x 15.5cm (6in x 6in) white felt
- 20cm x 15.5cm (8in x 6in) gold felt
- 30cm x 9cm (12in x 3½in) yellow felt
- Scraps of printed cotton fabrics for the appliqué

- Small handful of polyester stuffing
- 1.5m (1¾yd) red and yellow narrow ric-rac for buntings
- 2.25m (2½yd) green wide ric-rac
- 2.25m (2½yd) ready-made binding
- Buttons: four black micro, six yellow small, one yellow large, two gold small, two red heart-shaped and six balloon-shaped in assorted colours
- One large popper
- Embroidery threads: yellow, black, red, white, green
- Seven lengths of 5mm (¼in) wide assorted braids each measuring 11.5cm (4½in)
- Two pieces of transparent plastic measuring 7cm x 5.5cm (2¾in x 2¼in)
- Two pieces of card measuring 7cm x 5.5cm (2¾in x 2¼in)
- 25.5cm (10in) length of wooden dowel

Finished size: 49.5cm x 73.7cm (19½in x 29in)

Prepare the fabrics

1. Cut white cotton fabric into seven pieces measuring 11.5cm x 24.2cm (4½in x 9½in) for the bed sheets.

2. Cut the denim background fabric into the following pieces:

Four pieces 5.1cm x 14cm (2in x 5½in)

Four pieces 29.4cm x 5.1cm (15½in x 2in)

Two pieces 8.8cm x 16.5cm (3½in x 6½in)

Two pieces 15.3cm x 14cm (6in x 5½in)

Two pieces 6.5cm x 70cm (2½in x 27½in)

Two pieces 11.5cm x 16.5cm (4½in x 6½in)

One piece 49.5cm x 5cm (19½in x 2in)

3. Cut the green striped fabric into the following pieces:

One piece 25.5cm x 16.5cm (10in x 6½in)

Two pieces 11.5cm x 16.5cm (4½in x 6½in)

Make and assemble the bed rows

1. To make a little bed refer to Fig. 1 as you work. Sew one piece of the bedspread fabric to one piece of the sheet fabric. Press the seam towards the bedspread fabric. Fold over and press 2.5cm (1in) of the sheet at the top of the bedspread. Where the sheet meets the bottom of the bedspread, fold and press it back up to make the bottom sheet. Repeat to make the six other beds.

2. Lay the beds out in two rows of three with one at the top, adjusting the arrangement until you are happy the colours go together well.

3. Unfold the beds ready to add the bedspread decorations. Working on the front of the fabric, add decorative tapes, ribbon or ric-rac of your choosing to decorate the edge of the sheet turnover where it meets the bedspread. Trace the numbers 1 to 7 (see Templates) onto the fusible webbing (note the numbers are reversed). Fuse the numbers onto the wrong side of the white felt following the instructions for working with fusible webbing (see Get Ready to Stitch). Appliqué the numbers onto the bedspreads starting with 7 on the top bed. Refold the beds and pin the fold. Lay the beds back out in number order.

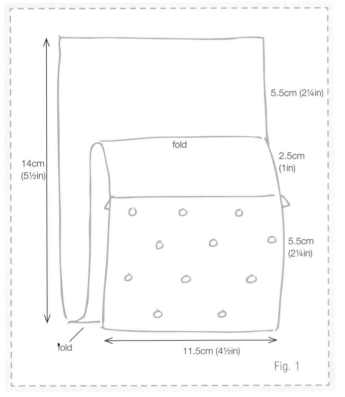

Fig. 1

4. Starting with the two rows of three beds, sew the beds together with a 5.1cm x 14cm (2in x 5½in) denim strip in between each bed. Press the seams to one side.

5. For the single bed row, sew the two 15.3cm x 14cm (6in x 5½in) rectangles to either side of the number 7 bed.

6. Join the three bed rows together with two of the 29.4cm x 5.1cm (15½in x 2in) denim strips. Sew the remaining 29.4cm x 5.1cm (15½in x 2in) strips to the top of the hanging and to the bottom bed row.

When working through several layers, pin well and sew slowly, using a walking foot attachment for your machine if you have one.

Appliqué the birthday party scene and complete the assembly

1. Following the open-door photograph as your guide, appliqué the central birthday party scene to the large piece of green stripe fabric. (For the tablecloth, birthday cake, balloons and bunting, see Templates; for the presents cut two rectangles from your fabric scraps; note the birthday scene will be completed when you add the doors later.) Secure the appliqué with hand or machine blanket stitch. Sew on the narrow

yellow ric-rac to join the bunting flags. The remaining stitching will be added later when quilting the wall hanging.

2. Sew the two denim pieces measuring 8.8cm x 16.5cm (3½in x 6½in) to either side of the birthday party scene. Press the seams to one side and then sew this strip to the bottom of the beds.

3. Sew the two denim strips measuring 6.5cm x 70cm (2½in x 27½in) to either side of the wall hanging; press the seams to one side and then add the final 49.5cm x 5cm (19½in x 2in) strip to the bottom of the hanging; press well.

4. To make the house shape at the top of the hanging, measure and mark 12.8cm (5in) in along the top and down the side on each of the corners. Join the marks up with a ruler and cut off.

5. Referring to Templates appliqué the waiting dog and three balloons onto the denim to the left-hand side of the party scene and the pennant to the right-hand side using hand or machine blanket stitch. (Note: embroidery details and embellishments will be added later.)

When appliquéing such small pieces, if working by hand use a small sharp needle, or if working by machine use a very fine needle, either 80/12 or 70/10.

Make the name and date holders

1. Use the name/date holder template to cut two rectangles from yellow felt and use fusible webbing to fuse together. Mark on the aperture (dotted line on template) and cut out. Repeat to make a second holder. Place the pieces of plastic behind the apertures on the holders and place this onto scrap paper. Machine stitch close to the inside edge. (The paper prevents the plastic from sticking to the machine and is torn away once the stitching is complete.) Blanket stitch along the top edge of the holder using two strands of red embroidery thread.

2. Pin the holders to either side of the top bed and blanket stitch in place by hand. Appliqué a fabric heart on either side of bed number 7, just above the holders, and blanket stitch by hand.

Quilt the wall hanging

1. Layer up the front, the wadding (batting) and the lining fabric (see Techniques: Making a quilt sandwich).

2. Stitch-in-the-ditch around each of the beds: you can either choose to do this by hand or by using a sewing machine with a walking foot attachment. Then if you are confident with your sewing, machine stitch 6mm (¼in) away from the edge.

3. Machine stitch around the name and date holders, keeping the top edge unstitched so you can change the child's name and date as appropriate. Hand-stitch a running stitch outline around the hearts and

the balloons using two strands of red thread. Cut a 7.5cm (3in) piece of narrow ric-rac and attach it with two small heart-shaped buttons to the top of the pennant at either side to make a 'hanger', following the photograph as your guide. Backstitch the strings of the balloons. (Note: the dog is embroidered later.)

4. Make a cardboard template measuring 10cm x 5cm (4in x 2in). Use the template to mark a pillow onto each of the beds, then embroider with a variety of stitches: chain, blanket, running stitch and backstitch have been used.

Make the doors

1. Appliqué the banners (see Templates) to the front of the remaining two pieces of denim measuring 11.5cm x 16.5cm (4½in x 6½in), positioning them 5cm (2in) down from the top edge.

2. Cut two pieces of interfacing measuring 15.5cm x 10cm (6in x 4in) and spray glue to the wrong side of the remaining green stripe lining fabric, making sure it is positioned centrally on the fabric.

3. On one of the door lining pieces, appliqué the three balloons, bunting flag and party dog wearing his party hat and scarf (see Templates). On the other door, appliqué the musical chairs and the bunting flags. (When positioning the bunting flags, make sure they will line up with the bunting on the central party scene.) Sew on the narrow yellow ric-rac along the top of the bunting flags.

Embellish and quilt the party scene

1. Chain stitch in white for the highlights on the balloons, in blue for the candles, and in yellow for the candle flames. Backstitch the balloon strings in red, the dog's mouth in black, the dog's arms and leg definition in white. Work a French knot in black for the dog's eye. Sew a small yellow button on top of the dog's hat. Quilt around the bunting flags, tablecloth, presents and balloons with a long running stitch using red thread.

2. Embroider the musical notes with backstitch and French knots. Sew around the chairs with red backstitch, adding the line details as marked on the templates. Satin stitch the dog's nose in black.

Attach the doors

1. Place a denim and green stripe door together with right sides facing and stitch immediately next to the interfacing, but not on it, and leaving the hinge side of each door unsewn. Clip the corners and turn the right way out. Press.

It's a really lovely idea to personalize your quilt by appliquéing or embroidering on the child's name.

2. Place the 1.3cm (½in) tape on the hinge (raw edge) of the door front, just covering the raw edges. Pin and sew the edge of the tape that is furthest away from the raw edge. Place the doors in position; pin and sew all the way around the tape (including the edge you have just sewn) through all layers of the hanging.

3. Sew on a heart-shaped button handle half way down the left-hand door. Sew two 1.3cm (½in) bar tacks (see Techniques: Making bar tacks), one on the opening edge of each door half way down. Sew on a group of three balloon buttons above the banners on the front of each door and chain stitch the balloon strings with red thread.

Add the final embellishments

1. To add the bunting beneath each row of beds, cut 36 triangles for the flags from your fabric scraps. Draw slightly wiggly lines to mark the position of the bunting strings across the quilt. Pin on 12 flags along each line and then sew them in place with a straight line of stitching

close to the top edge of the flags. Place the narrow ric-rac over the stitching line and sew in place. Sew a small yellow button at the end of each string of bunting.

2. Fold back each door and mark the position to sew a button on to fasten the door back.

3. Embroider a running stitch border at the base of the tablecloth. Sew a backstitch red ribbon using two strands of embroidery thread on one of the presents and top with a red ribbon bow. Sew white ric-rac to the other present and top with a white ric-rac bow. Sew a yellow star stitch for the cake decoration.

4. Sew a small red heart-shaped button onto the dog's present and the large yellow button in the middle of the top row. Sew one half of the large popper to the right of the table just above the presents.

5. Bind the wall hanging (see Techniques: Using ready-made binding).

Make Bertie the bear

1. Use the Bertie the bear pattern (see Templates) to trace one bear body and two arms onto freezer paper (if you have it) or plain paper (if you don't); cut them out.

2. Fold the piece of gold felt in half. If you are using freezer paper, iron the pieces onto the felt; if you are using plain paper, pin the patterns onto the felt. DO NOT CUT OUT. Machine stitch all the way around the body and arm templates, close to the edge and leaving no gaps. Neatly cut very close to the stitching line.

3. Hand blanket stitch all the way around the body and arms using two strands of embroidery floss or one strand of coton à broder.

4. Cut a slit in one layer of the bear's neck and arms as indicated on the patterns, gently stuff with a little polyester stuffing, then stitch the opening closed.

5. Cut a muzzle from a single layer of felt and blanket stitch onto Bertie's face. Embroider the nose and mouth with two strands of black thread. Sew two black micro buttons on for his eyes.

6. Using the two remaining small yellow buttons, sew Bertie's arms to the front shoulders. Sew the other half of the large popper between Bertie's shoulder blades on his back.

7. Using the pattern, cut a scarf from red polka dot fabric and tie it around Bertie's neck.

Make the hanging loops

1. The hanging loops have been designed to look like two little chimneys to complete Bertie's house. Cut two 5cm x 15.5cm (2in x 6in) rectangles from red fabric and two 7.5cm x 15.5cm (3in x 6in) from denim fabric.

2. Place a red and denim rectangle right sides together, match one side seam, and sew down this side. Match the other side seam – the denim will appear too big at this stage – and sew. Turn the right way out – the denim will appear to wrap itself around the red fabric. Press.

3. Fold the chimneys in half denim side facing and sew them to the back of the wall hanging 4cm (1½in) from each edge.

4. Take the wooden dowel and thread it through the chimney loops. Your finished wall hanging is now ready to be hung.

Christmas

I love to decorate my home at Christmas, as those who have my previous books will know. It is a little bit of an addiction and my love of all things homemade comes to the forefront in the festive season.

I adore the feisty robin with his bright red breast and his bold nature – he has no qualms about coming right up close to me as he waits for me to uncover bugs as I garden. So it's no surprise that the robin motif features so strongly in this celebration chapter, along with a selection of seasonal motifs.

There's a robin pennant to hang on your door to welcome your guests, robin decorations to hang from the tree, and a robin wine glass lampshade to brighten your mantelpiece. A second lampshade design features a crazy-patchwork redwork embroidery design and this is adapted to also make a super mini bunting for the Christmas tree.

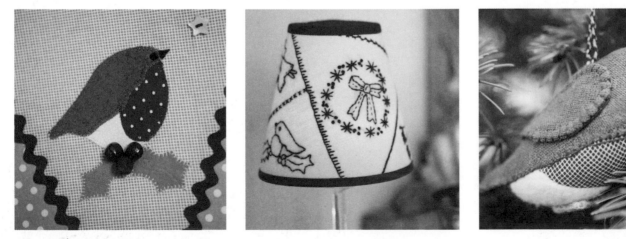

Christmas Lampshades

Create a bit of magic at the Christmas table with these seasonal lampshades that are cleverly designed to sit atop wine glasses, which are safely illuminated with battery night lights. There are two different styles to choose from: a sweet little appliquéd robin or a crazy patchwork embroidery of Christmas motifs in festive red.

To make the embroidered lampshade

1. Using the lampshade template supplied (see Templates: Top Table Lampshades), trace off the outline onto a folded piece of paper as marked and cut out. Open up the paper pattern and glue it onto thin card to give you your full lampshade template.

2. Mark around the template onto thick iron-on interfacing; cut out and set aside. Place the template in the middle of the linen fabric and draw around it using a pencil.

3. Transfer the embroidery design (see Templates) onto the front of the fabric, and then iron the lightweight interfacing onto the wrong side of the fabric, centring it over the embroidered design.

4. Stitch the embroidery design using two strands of thread, starting first with the dividing lines, working from left to right as follows: whipped running stitch, cross stitch, blanket stitch (alternating the length of the stitches), another row of whipped running stitch, and herringbone stitch.

7. Bind around the outside edge of the lampshade using the ready-made binding starting at one of the top corners and mitring the corners (see Techniques: Using ready-made binding).

8. Mark on the button positions along one side edge, and make the bar tacks on the opposite side (see Techniques: Making bar tacks). Finally, sew on the four small red buttons.

You will need for the robin appliqué lampshade

- 30cm x 20cm (12in x 8in) background fabric
- Scraps of red, brown and white for the robin appliqué
- 30cm x 20cm (12in x 8in) thick iron-on interfacing
- Fusible webbing
- Threads to match appliqué fabrics
- Stranded cotton (floss): brown and black
- Four small red buttons
- One black micro button
- 1m (40in) of 2cm (¾in) ready-made binding

Finished size: 33cm x 10cm (13in x 4in)

5. Now embroider the motifs within the crazy-patchwork design sections. Use backstitch for the outlines of the heart, the angel, the robin and the holly, the bow within the wreath, the snowman, and the star and the tree. Use French knots for the angel's hair, the robin's eye, the holly berries on the wreath, the snowman's eyes and mouth and at the top of the fringe of his scarf, and for the points of the star and the decorations on the tree. Finish the heart with blanket stitch. Use star stitch for the angel's swag, the wreath, the snowman's nose and bobble on his hat, and for the star on the top of the tree. Use running stitch to add the details to the hem of the angel's dress, to the holly leaves, to the bow on the wreath, and to the snowman's hat.

6. Once you have finished the embroidery, press the fabric well. Iron or spray glue the thick interfacing onto the wrong side of your work, making sure the embroidery design is centralized in it. Trim the linen fabric to the size of the interfacing.

To make the robin appliqué lampshade

1. Follow steps 1 and 2 for the embroidered lampshade. Working with the fusible webbing (see Get Ready to Stitch) appliqué the robin motif onto the middle of the background fabric, using a scrap of brown fabric for the body, white for the belly and red for the breast (see Templates: Christmas Pennant). Blanket stitch by machine using threads to match the fabrics. (Alternatively, blanket stitch by hand using two strands of stranded cotton [floss] or coton à broder.)

2. Embroider the feet by hand using a backstitch and two strands of stranded cotton (floss). Sew on a micro button for the eye and embroider on a beak in black using satin stitch.

3. Iron or spray glue the thick interfacing onto the wrong side of your work, making sure the appliquéd design is centralized in it. Trim the linen fabric to the size of the interfacing.

4. To complete the lampshade, follow steps 7 and 8 for the embroidered lampshade.

Mini Tree Bunting

I love bunting for any occasion and I think it works really well as a miniature garland used to decorate the Christmas tree. The white and red stand out beautifully against the dark green of the tree and it is easy to attach with mini clips. It also makes a great Christmas gift.

1. Using the mini bunting flag supplied (see Templates), trace off the pattern outline onto paper, glue it onto thin card, and cut out on the line to give you your bunting template. Use the card template to mark out five flags onto one piece of your linen fabric using a fadeaway or washable pen and leaving 5cm (2in) in between each flag.

2. Using the Christmas Lampshades embroidery design (see Templates), trace one of the five Christmas designs (excluding the heart motif) in the centre of each flag; do not worry if the designs go over the edge. Iron the lightweight interfacing to the back of the fabric.

3. Backstitch the Christmas motif outlines, and then add the finer details. Work a circle of star stitches for the Christmas wreath adding a cluster of three French knot 'berries' in between. Add lines of running stitch to the ribbon tails. Add a French knot eye to the robin. Work a French knot bauble at the end of each of the tree's branches and add a star stitch to the top of the tree. Work a mass of French knots for the angel's hair and a gentle curve of star stitches between the hands for the garland.

> It's easier to embroider the small flags as a larger piece of work, and once finished cut them to the correct size.

You will need

- Two pieces of white linen each measuring 15.5cm x 40.5cm (6in x 16in)
- 15.5cm x 46cm (6in x 18in) lightweight iron-on interfacing
- 60cm (23½in) of 1.3cm (½in) wide ribbon
- Four small red bells
- Red coton à broder
- Clips for hanging

Finished size: 60cm x 10cm (23½in x 4in)

4. For the snowman, work French knots for his eyes and nose and a star stitch nose. Add a star stitch bobble to the top of his hat and running stitch borders to the hatband. To complete his scarf, work French knots to the tops of the scarf fringing. Add a scattering of star stitches to the background of each flag to finish the embroidery.

5. Once the embroidery is complete, turn the fabric over and use your card template to mark the flags over the embroidered designs. Place the embroidered fabric on top of the second piece of linen fabric, right sides together, and machine stitch over the marked lines, leaving the tops of the flags open. Cut out around the flags, trim the seams, and turn through the right way. Press and carefully pick the tip of the triangle out with a pin.

6. Sew a running stitch border around the inside edge of each of the completed flags.

7. Lay the ribbon right side down on your work surface. Starting 10cm (4in) from the left-hand edge, place a flag with the embroidered side facing down so that the unstitched top aligns with the centre line of the ribbon. Leaving a 2.5cm (1in) gap, pin the second flag in place onto the ribbon as before. Repeat to pin the remaining flags in place, ending with a 10cm (4in) length of ribbon or tape at the right-hand side.

8. Using a thread that matches the ribbon, machine stitch the flags in place close to the edge of the ribbon. Fold the ribbon over to the back of the flags and slip stitch by hand. Sew together the edges of the ribbon lengths at either end with a machine or hand running stitch. Thread a clip on at each end of the ribbon; fold over the ribbon ends and sew in place to secure. Sew on the jingle bells between each flag to finish.

I have used East of India tape to sew the flags together but any cotton ribbon will do. Dressmaker's binding works a treat too but will not be as decorative.

The ribbon lengths left at either end of the garland are long enough to allow you to tie the bunting to the tree if you are not using clips.

Christmas Pennant

A Christmas pennant makes a great alternative to a wreath – just hang it on your front door to welcome guests to your home during the festive season. You will need a sturdy hanger to keep it in place and a fabric-covered wooden dowel is ideal.

1. Make a standard pennant (see Pennants) using a small green check as the background fabric.

2. Iron fusible webbing to the wrong side of the green spot fabric and cut three 5cm x 46cm (2in x 18in) strips from it. Peel the backing paper of the strips and iron them onto the top and both side edges of the pennant, overlap at all three corners. Trim. Blanket stitch in place by machine or by hand.

3. Place the red ric-rac over the inside edge of the green dot and stitch through the middle of the ric-rac.

4. Following the instructions for fusible webbing (see Get Ready to Stitch), appliqué the robin and holly (see Templates) in place, using the photograph as a guide for colours. Sew on a micro button or small bead for an eye and embroider a beak in black using satin stitch.

5. Fuse the backing fabric to the wrong side of the pennant. Bind all three edges with the ready-made binding.

6. Sew on the three star-shaped buttons to the right of the robin and three red bells to the holly. Sew the ribbon bow onto the bottom tip of the inside triangle and sew the two red medium-sized buttons at either side of the top of the inside triangle.

7. To cover the dowel, fold the red fabric in half along its length, right sides together. Sew the long seam with a 6mm (¼in) seam allowance, leaving the short ends open. Turn the fabric tube the right way out, thread it onto the dowel and gather it up.

You will need

- 23cm x 46cm (9in x 18in) green dot fabric
- 25.5cm x 23cm (10in x 9in) green check fabric
- 59cm x 7.5cm (23in x 3in) red fabric
- 35.5cm x 40.5cm (14in x 16in) backing fabric
- Scraps of brown, red, white and green fabric for the appliqué
- 50cm (20in) fusible webbing
- 76cm (30in) red narrow ric-rac
- Ribbon bow
- Three small bells
- One black micro button
- Three small white star-shaped buttons
- Two red medium-sized buttons
- Two small pom poms
- 33cm (13in) length of wooden dowel
- 120cm (47in) of 2cm (¾in) ready-made binding
- 50cm (20in) hanging cord

Finished size: 33cm x 37cm (13in x 14½in)

8. To make the hanging loops, cut two 13cm (5in) pieces of the binding. Take one piece and fold it right sides together. Sew it to the top, wrong side of the pennant, 5cm (2in) in from the side. Repeat for the other piece.

9. Thread the dowel through the hanging loops and glue a pom pom to each end. Tie the length of cord to each end of the dowel to enable you to hang up the pennant.

Robin Decorations

There is no sight more cheery than a perky little robin redbreast. This little bird will need a good deal of stuffing to puff out his bright chest. Make a flock and hang them from a twisted willow branch, covered in twinkling lights.

....

1. Use the robin pattern (see Templates) to cut out: two bodies, four wings and one tail from brown fabric/felt; one breast from red fabric/felt; one belly from white fabric/felt; one beak and two feet from yellow felt.

2. Place the bodies right sides together and sew from A to B only, using a 6mm (¼in) seam allowance and stitching by machine, or by hand with very small backstitches, using matching thread.

3. Place the red breast on top of the white belly so it overlaps at the seam and tack (baste) in place. Blanket stitch the two pieces together by hand. Sew the tail to the other end of the belly.

4. Insert the joined breast/belly/tail piece into the main body, matching and pinning point A to the tail with a little nip and tucking. Sew all the way around leaving NO gap for turning through (see step 6).

5. Pair the wings together, right sides facing, and stitch all the way around the edge, leaving NO turning gap. Make a slit in the inside layer only of each sewn wing (take care not to make the slits on the same side of each wing). Turn the wings to the right side through the slits, and then sew the slits closed. Sew around the edge of each wing with blanket stitch.

6. To turn the robin's body through to the right side, make a slit on one side of the bird's body where one of the wings will be positioned (the wing will hide the sewn up slit). Turn inside out and stuff with polyester stuffing paying particular attention to the breast. Make sure the robin is really firm, squashing the body around in your hands to get a nice shape. Sew the slit closed with ladder stitch (see Techniques: Utility stitches). Apply fabric glue to the open side of the wings, then attach to either side of the robin's body making sure to cover the turning slit.

7. Embroider over the body seams with blanket stitch, then sew a micro button eye on either side of the robin's head pulling the thread up tightly to get an indentation for the eye socket.

8. Glue or sew the beak onto the robin's head and the feet beneath the body. Sew a length of decorative cord or a thin piece of ribbon to the back of the bird for hanging.

Celebration Quilt

Friendship quilts, made from repeat blocks that were then signed by the makers, have been around for over 200 years. The quilts were made in many different patterns, from simple repeat blocks to the famous Baltimore-album style of friendship quilt, which were individually created blocks sometimes of great complexity.

While the modern twenty-first century woman has far less time to create such a masterpiece, the purpose of the friendship quilt – to record the sentiments and memories of cherished friends and family – is still very relevant today.

I designed this very simple quilt to be made from squares of fabric sewn together, quilted, then appliquéd with a bunting design. Embroider the bunting flags with a loving message for the most delightful present for a wedding, anniversary or special birthday. You could even make a separate celebration bunting to match.

Friendship Quilt

The more meaningful the collection of fabrics used, the better; ask friends and family to donate sentimental fabrics. Dish out the bunting flags to be signed by loved ones, then embroidered, before the quilt's construction, or get them signed at the party and embroider later. Either way use an indelible pen that will not bleed or fade.

1. Lightly spray starch all your fabrics before starting work. Note, the backing fabric will require halving and joining. Cut 64 squares measuring 14cm (5½in) from the printed fabrics. It is important to make these exactly the same size; if you do not cut them out well the quilt may be difficult to put together. Use a rotary cutter and ruler; alternatively make a cardboard template the exact size and mark around the template onto the fabric, and then cut out very neatly.

2. Lay out the squares in eight rows of eight squares, making sure that the same fabrics are not touching each other. Sew each row together with a 6mm (¼in) seam, or use the width of your machine foot as a guide. Press the first seam of the first row to the left, then the next row's seam to the right, so that when the rows are joined they will butt up to each other. Pin well before you sew the long rows.

3. Measure your quilt top through the middle and cut two borders to this length, joining fabric strips as necessary. Pin each end of the border strip to the quilt top, then pin well in between. Sew, then press seams to one side.

4. Measure the quilt top from border to border, again through the middle, and cut the remaining two border strips to this length (again, fabric strips will need joining). Pin and sew as before.

5. Make a quilt sandwich by layering up the pieced quilt top, the wadding (batting) and the backing (see Techniques: Making a quilt sandwich), and machine quilt using a vermicelli pattern.

6. Using fusible webbing and the medium bunting pattern (see Templates), cut out 19 flags from the white fabric. Lay the quilt

You will need

- 16 pieces of printed fabric 30cm (12in) square
- 77cm (30in) of 107cm (42in) wide fabric for borders
- 2.5m (2¾yd) of 107cm (42in) wide fabric for backing
- 50cm (20in) of 107cm (42in) wide white fabric for bunting flags
- 40cm (16in) of 107cm (42in) wide fabric for binding
- 1m (1⅛yd) fusible webbing
- 138cm x 138cm (54in x 54in) wadding (batting)
- Wide ric-rac: 9m (10yd) white and 4m (4⅜yd) green
- 38 small and five large buttons
- Permanent, non-fade, archival quality pen (I use Micron pigma pens 0.5 width)

Finished size: 127.5cm x 127.5cm (50in x 50in)

patchwork side up, and roughly pin on the green ric-rac so that the bunting will swag across it. Lay the flags out along the ric-rac line and pin them in place, temporarily removing the ric-rac as you do so. Once you are satisfied with the layout of the flags, peel off the backing paper and iron in position, flag by flag. To secure the flags in place, hand or machine blanket stitch around each, then hand quilt a running stitch 6mm (¼in) in from the outside edge.

7. Re-pin the green ric-rac and sew straight down the middle of it with matching thread. Pin and sew the white ric-rac to the border seam in the same way. Sew a small white button to each side of the top of each flag and large white buttons to each end of the bunting swags. Use the remaining white ric-rac to decorate the outside edge of the quilt before binding (see Techniques: Making a double-bound edge). Get friends and family to sign the flags, then embroider over the signatures with backstitch using one strand of embroidery thread.

Pennants

A pennant is a great way to celebrate a once-in-a-lifetime event and makes a wonderful keepsake of the celebration, from a special birthday such as an 18th or 21st, to a couple's wedding day. Pennants also make a great addition to party bunting, and celebration pennants can be brought out each year to celebrate all the most important calendar events, including Easter and Christmas. The Christmas Pennant is sewn for a more permanent finish, but when time is short you can make a pennant decoration with just a few quick snips, a bit of pasting, and a little hand embroidered stitching.

To make a standard pennant

1 Make a cardboard template from lightweight card. Draw a 33cm (13in) line across the top of card and mark the centre point. From the centre point, draw a line 37cm (14½in) down. Join the bottom of the vertical line up with each end of the horizontal line to give you a triangle. Cut out your triangle template.

2. Use the template to cut out a triangle from your chosen background fabric, backing fabric, thick interfacing or blackout lining, and two triangles from fusible webbing.

3. Fuse the background fabric triangle onto the thick interfacing triangle. If decorating your pennant with an appliqué design, fuse your chosen celebration design onto the background fabric (see Get Ready to Stitch: Working the Appliqué). Fusible webbing will glue the design down but if you intend to use the pennant time and time again, it will need to be stitched to keep it in place more permanently, either by hand or by machine blanket stitch.

4. Fuse the backing fabric onto the pennant. Decorate the edges of the pennant: choose from ribbon, decorative tapes, ric-rac, bobble braid and binding, or use trimmings in combination. The trims can be glued, fused or sewn in place. To bind the edges of the pennant with a coordinating ready-made binding, follow the instructions in Techniques; the trims can be glued, fused or sewn in place.

You will need

- 35.5cm x 40.5cm (14in x 16in) background fabric
- 35.5cm x 40.5cm (14in x 16in) backing fabric
- 35.5cm x 40.5cm (14in x 16in) thick interfacing or blackout lining
- 35.5cm x 82cm (14in x 32in) fusible webbing
- Scraps of fabric and fusible webbing for appliqué
- Ribbon, decorative tapes, bobble braid, ric-rac and ready-made binding for trimming
- Button decorations
- Wooden dowel

Finished size: 33cm x 37cm (13in x 14½in)

5. To make a casing for the wooden dowel, sew a strip of binding to the top back edge of the pennant, keeping both ends open to thread the dowel through. Alternatively, make hanging loops to thread the dowel through (see Christmas Pennant). Decorate the dowel ends by gluing on buttons or similar trim, and tie a length of cord, ribbon or braid to the dowel to hang the pennant up.

You will need a 33cm (13in) length of wooden dowel if you choose to thread it through the tape at the back of the pennant or a 38cm (15in) length if the dowel is to protrude at each end of the pennant.

Pictured opposite, from top left clockwise:
- To make special birthday pennants use the Birthday Badge number templates enlarged by 200% and add an appliqué design of your choosing.
- A sweet hatching chick design makes a cheery decoration for Easter.
- Bobble braid is the perfect trim to decorate a pennant.
- Combine ric-rac and binding to create a striking border for your pennant.
- A pumpkin appliqué on a rustic check fabric background makes a great celebration pennant for Halloween or Thanksgiving. The pumpkin shape is defined with simple backstitch and fancy yarn has been used for the stalk.
- On the wedding pennant two felt dove appliqués 'carry' a mother-of-pearl button heart that has the initials of the bride and groom embroidered inside it.

Techniques

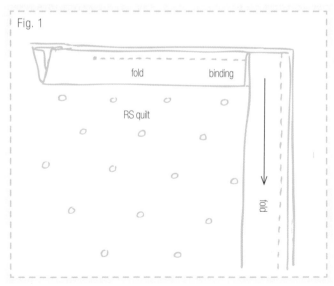

BINDING

Bindings decorate and finish a raw edge at the same time. The binding can be made using the project fabric as for the double-bound edge of the Friendship Quilt, or ready-made binding can be bought as for the Table Top Lampshades.

Making a double-bound edge

Cut your binding fabric into 6cm (2½in) fabric strips and join to form one continuous length. Press open the seams. Fold the joined strip in half lengthways and press. Working with the right side of the quilt facing you, lay the binding along one side, matching the raw edges. Start 7.5cm (3in) from the beginning of the binding, and sew using a generous 6mm (¼in) seam.

Fig. 1

fold   binding

RS quilt

fold

Stitch until you reach one corner, stopping EXACTLY 6mm (¼in) from the end. Pull the work away from the machine and fold the binding up so that it is aligned with the edge of the quilt, making sure it is straight. Holding the corner, fold the binding back down, aligning it with the raw edge and making sure that the folded corner is square. Pin and sew over the fold continuing down the next side as in Fig. 1.

Continue to bind around the quilt until you return to the starting point. Turn under 6mm (¼in) at the beginning of the binding. Place the end of the binding into the fold, trim to size and sew right over the top.

Fold the binding over to the back of the quilt and slip stitch in place. The corners will miraculously mitre for you on their own.

Using ready-made binding

There is no substitute for making your own binding especially when quilt making, but for smaller craft projects like bunting, pennants and lampshades the ready-made binding bought in haberdashery shops, available in a wide variety of colours and sizes. is ideal. It comes pre-folded and in some cases you can just place the raw edges of your project into the fold, pin and sew; sometimes the sewn line misses the fold on the back and you may have to slip stitch by hand. You can also use it by opening out all the folds on the binding to use it in the normal way, but you will have the advantage of using the fold lines as a guide.

UTILITY STITCHES

Perfect hand finishing stitches for a professional finish to your projects.

Ladder stitch

For closing a seam on a stuffed item or sewing two folded edges together. The stitches look like a ladder until they are pulled tight to close the seam. Knot the end of the thread and start from inside the opening to hide the knot. Take straight stitches into the folded fabric, stitching into each edge in turn. After a few stitches pull the thread taut to draw up the stitches and close the gap.

Slip stitch

Also used to close gaps in seams. When worked neatly, it is almost invisible. Work from right to left, picking up a tiny piece of the fabric from one seam edge. Insert the needle into the other seam fold and move the needle along 3mm (⅛in). Push the needle out into the seam edge and repeat.

MAKING BAR TACKS

This technique is required to make the button loops on the table lampshades. Sew three stitches on top of each other to match the width of the button you are using to fasten your shade with. Picking up the stitches only, sew along them with blanket stitches very close to each other to form a bar. Fasten off the thread to complete the bar tack.

SPRAY BASTING

For quick small craft projects I use a good brand of temporary spray adhesive in the place of tacking (basting) as it is quick and you can easily reposition your work. If you choose to do the same, always only spray the wadding (batting), never the work. Work surfaces have to be protected and you must read and follow the instructions on the can.

MAKING A QUILT SANDWICH

It is often said that 'quilting makes the quilt' and preparation is key to your success, so take your time with this part. Carefully press all the seams and cut off any stray threads. Cut a piece of backing fabric and a piece of cotton wadding (batting) at least 5cm (2in) bigger all aroundn than the quilt top. Lay the backing fabric on a flat surface wrong side facing you; smooth it out and secure it to the surface with a low-tack tape, ensuring that the fabric is perfectly flat and under a little tension. Lay the wadding (batting) on top and smooth out flat. Now place on the quilt top and smooth it out. Pin the layers of the quilt together, using safety pins every 7.5cm (3in). Start in the middle and work your way out to the edges. Do not scrimp on pins as this will lead to rucks and creases. Once pinned, tack (baste) all the way around the edge of the border. To stabilize the layered quilt, machine stitch-in-the-ditch around each block and along the borders using an inviible or matching thread. Then quilt with a decorative quilt pattern of your choosing.

EDGING WITH MEDIUM/WIDE RIC-RAC BRAID

I love ric-rac braid and often use it to edge my projects. It is available in different widths and the edging technique used differs slightly according to the ric-rac width used. When edging with medium/wide ric-rac it is important to position and machine the ric-rac carefully to prevent the humps of the ric-rac from disappearing when the project is turned the right way out. Working on the right side of the fabric, line up the edge of the ric-rac with the raw edge of the fabric. Tack (baste) in place by machine stitching down the middle of the ric-rac. When starting and finishing the edging keep the ends out of the way by tucking them back on themselves to leave the seam allowance ric-rac free (Fig. 2).

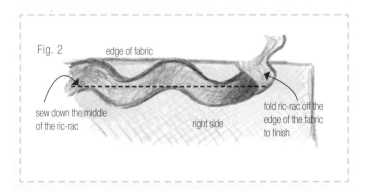

Fig. 2
edge of fabric
sew down the middle of the ric-rac
right side
fold ric-rac off the edge of the fabric to finish

Templates

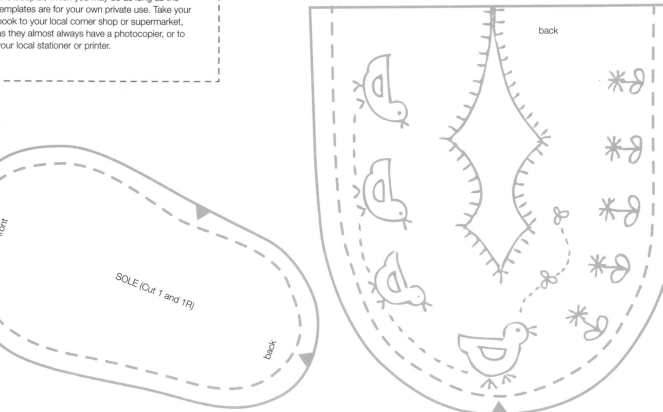

Note: Unless otherwise stated the templates on the following pages are the actual size you will need to make the projects. It will be necessary to enlarge a few of the templates by 200% on a photocopier, which you may do as long as the templates are for your own private use. Take your book to your local corner shop or supermarket, as they almost always have a photocopier, or to your local stationer or printer.

First Shoes

UPPER (Cut 2)

Note: Reverse the embroidery pattern for the right-hand shoe.

back

front

SOLE (Cut 1 and 1R)

back

Baby Sampler

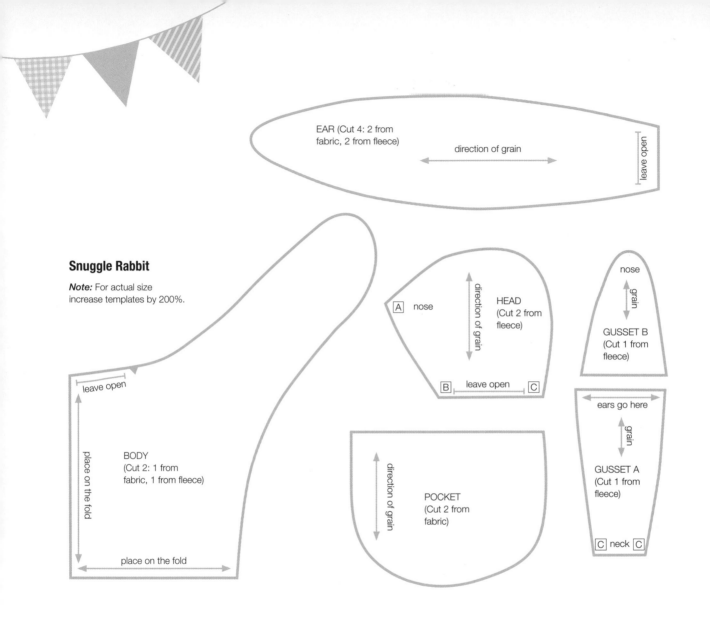

EAR (Cut 4: 2 from fabric, 2 from fleece)

direction of grain

leave open

Snuggle Rabbit

Note: For actual size increase templates by 200%.

A nose

HEAD (Cut 2 from fleece)

direction of grain

B leave open C

nose

grain

GUSSET B (Cut 1 from fleece)

leave open

BODY (Cut 2: 1 from fabric, 1 from fleece)

place on the fold

place on the fold

direction of grain

POCKET (Cut 2 from fabric)

ears go here

grain

GUSSET A (Cut 1 from fleece)

C neck C

Dribble Bibs

First Blanket

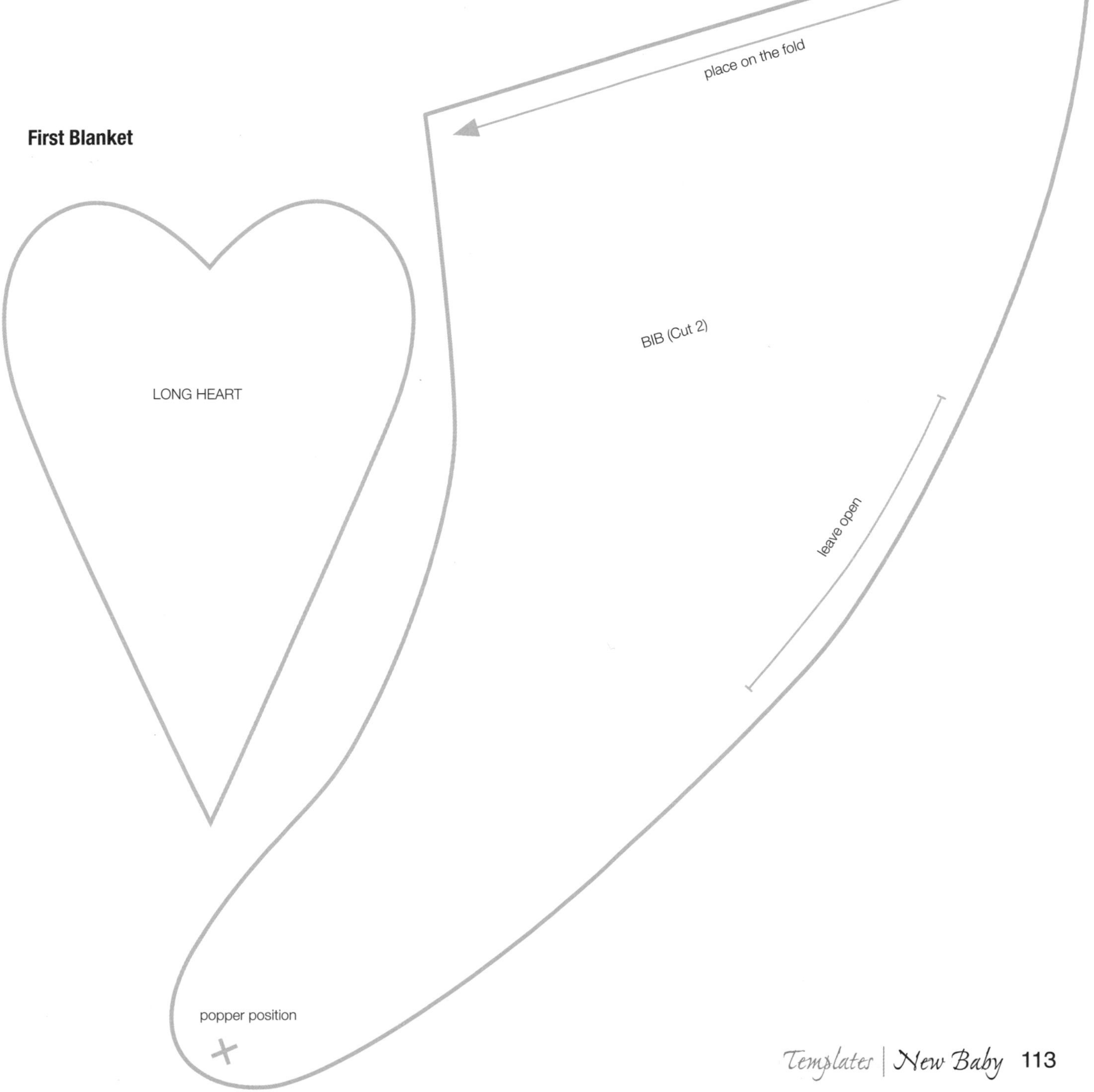

place on the fold

LONG HEART

BIB (Cut 2)

leave open

popper position

X

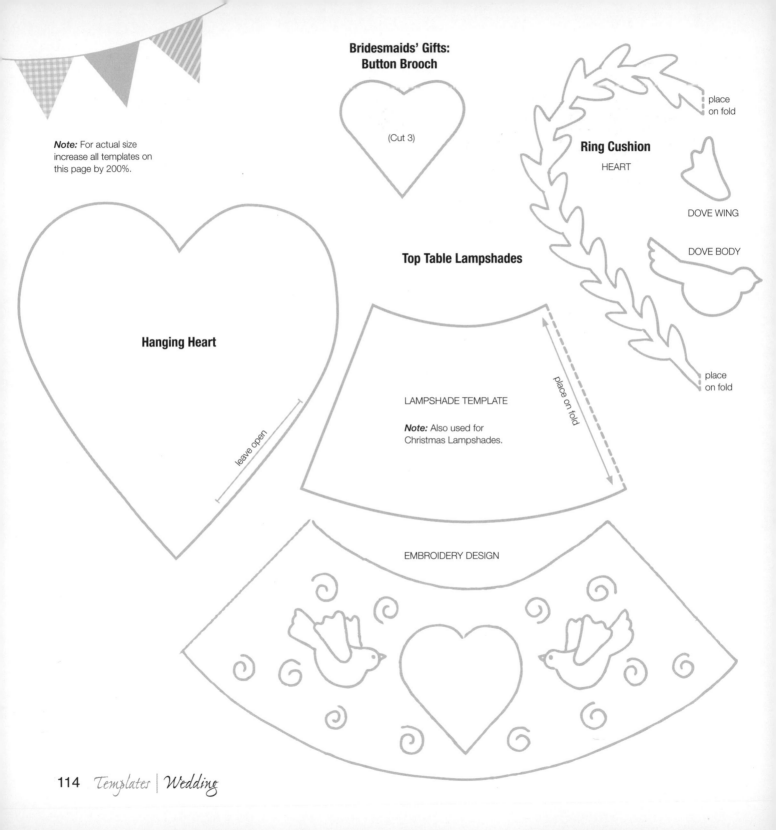

**Bridesmaids' Gifts:
Button Brooch**

(Cut 3)

Ring Cushion

HEART

place
on fold

DOVE WING

DOVE BODY

Note: For actual size
increase all templates on
this page by 200%.

Top Table Lampshades

place
on fold

Hanging Heart

leave open

LAMPSHADE TEMPLATE

Note: Also used for
Christmas Lampshades.

place on fold

EMBROIDERY DESIGN

Wedding Bunting

PENNANT

Crowns and Tiaras

Note: Trace off these templates onto folded pieces of paper to make the full patterns.

CROWN

TIARA

cut out

place on fold

place on fold

place on fold

place on fold

Birthday Badges

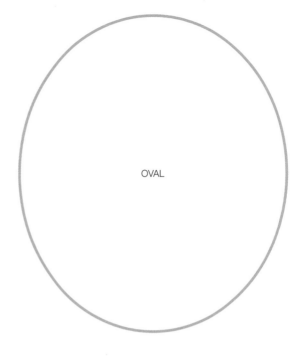

OVAL

NUMBERS
Note: The numbers can also be used
increased by 200% for the pennants.

Seven More Sleeps

PENNANT

BUNTING
(Cut 36)

HAT

BERTIE'S SCARF

MUZZLE

SCARF

cut to stuff

BERTIE
THE BEAR
BODY

PARTY DOG

cut to stuff

ARM
(Cut 2)

SCARF

PRESENT

BALLOONS
(Cut 9)

stitch
Line

WAITING DOG

TABLECLOTH

NAME/DATE HOLDER

BANNER

MUSICAL CHAIRS

BIRTHDAY CAKE

NUMBERS

1 2 3 4 5 6 7

Birthday Party Stitchery

Christmas Lampshades

Note: For actual size increase embroidery design by 200%. For lampshade template, see Wedding: Top Table Lampshades.

EMBROIDERY DESIGN

Christmas Pennant

Note: These templates are also used for the Christmas Lampshades.

Robin Decorations

Note: For actual size increase templates by 200%.

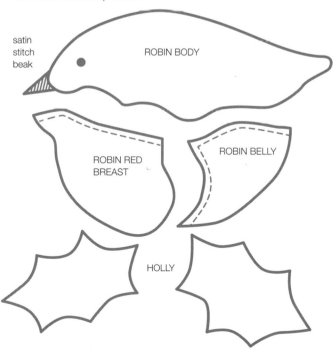

satin stitch beak

ROBIN BODY

ROBIN RED BREAST

ROBIN BELLY

HOLLY

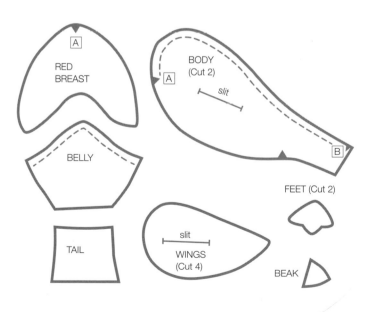

RED BREAST
A

BODY
(Cut 2)
A
slit
B

BELLY

FEET (Cut 2)

TAIL

slit
WINGS
(Cut 4)

BEAK

Bunting

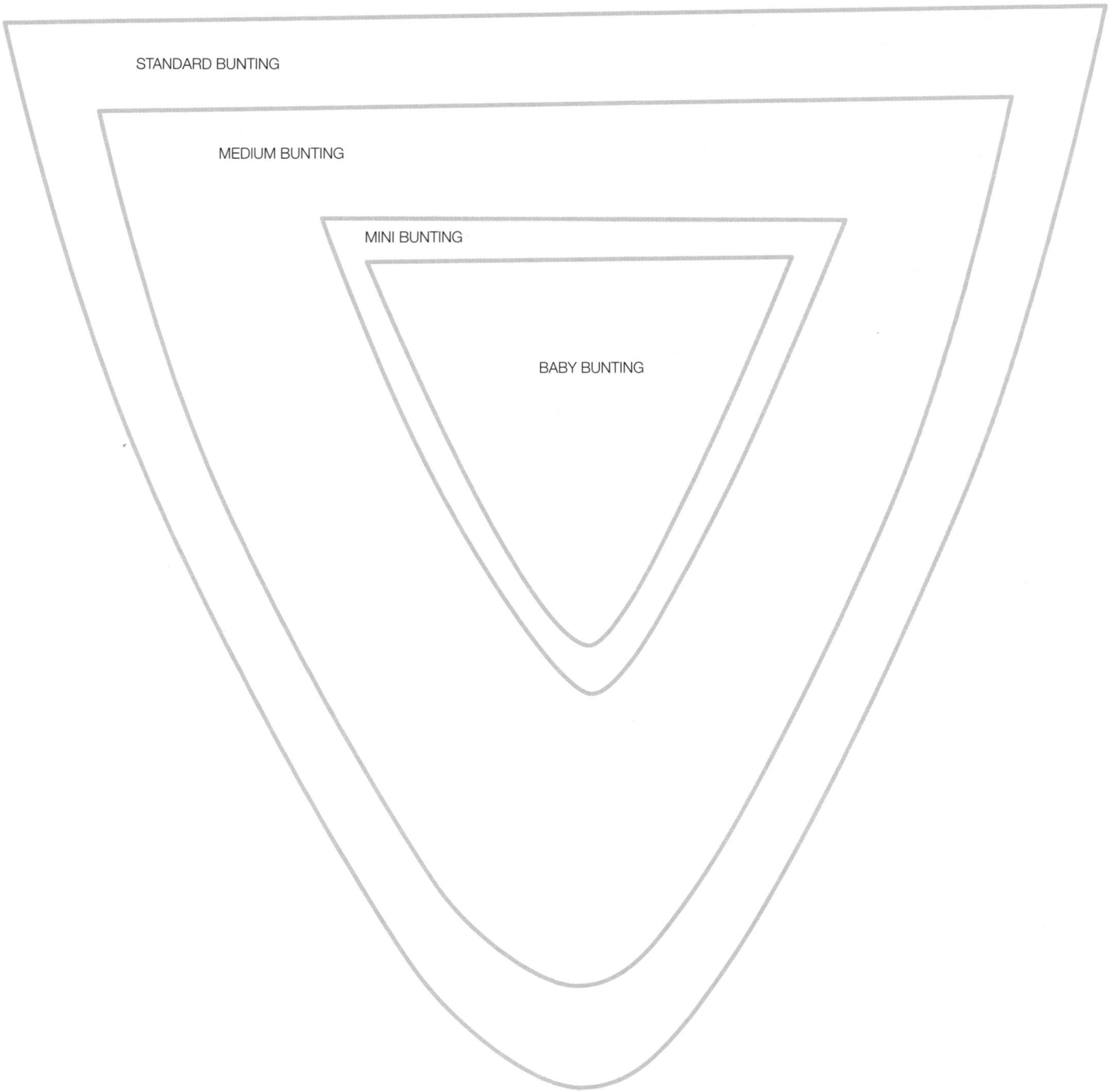

STANDARD BUNTING

MEDIUM BUNTING

MINI BUNTING

BABY BUNTING

Chick Pennant

Key to the Door Pennant

HEAD

× eye

BODY

SHELL

× button

Sweet 16 Pennant

Pumpkin Pennant

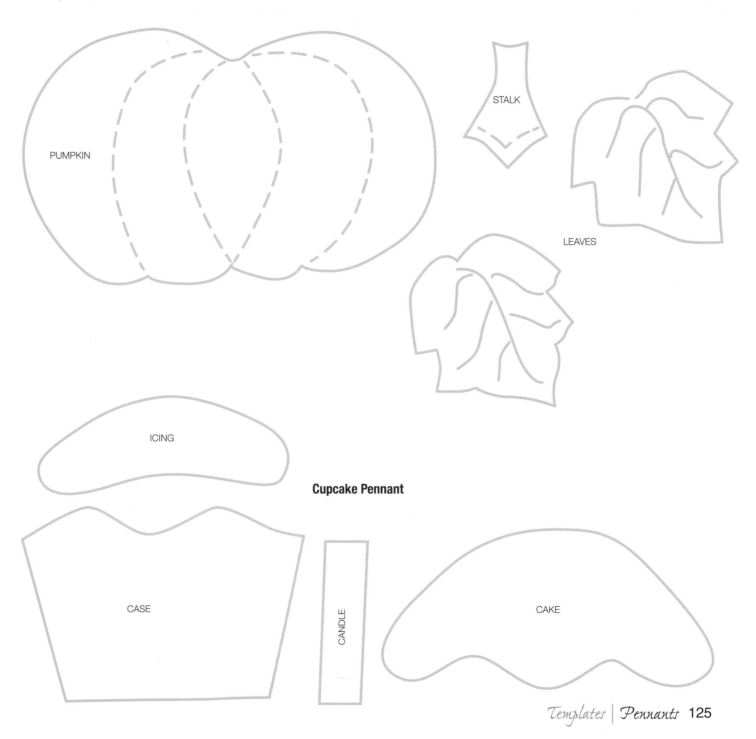

PUMPKIN

STALK

LEAVES

ICING

Cupcake Pennant

CASE

CANDLE

CAKE

Acknowledgments

Without the support of all of my friends, students and wonderful family, these creative works would not be possible. They keep me on a steady track within my creative mess and muddle, and help me to produce these projects and words that the magical team at David & Charles turn into the most beautiful books, which make my designs shine. Thank you to you all. xxxx

About the Author

Mandy Shaw describes herself as a maker of all things lovely, and she loves to share her inspirations with you. This will be her fourth book for David & Charles, and her ideas are still flowing. She lives in East Sussex in her homemade home with her large family and continues to teach and travel around the UK to share her passion for sewing crafts. She has appeared on Kirstie Allsopp's TV shows and contributed to two of Kirstie's books.

Mandy is a guest presenter on Create and Craft TV and frequently contributes to craft and patchwork magazines across the globe.

Suppliers

UK

www.dandeliondesigns.co.uk
Supplier of Mandy's patterns and kits and lots of fabric and haberdashery items related to Mandy's books including tapes, ric-rac, Fast2Fuse, felt, coton à broder and other threads.

www.liberty.co.uk/lifestylefabrics
New range of art fabrics including Bloomsbury Garden English florals.

www.makeruk.com
A good range of spots, checks and stripes.

www.roc-lon.com
Blackout curtain lining for pennants.

www.patchworkdogandbasket.co.uk
For patchwork and quilting fabrics, buttons, tapes and haberdashery.

www.thequiltroom.co.uk

www.cottonpatch.co.uk

www.stitchcraftcreate.co.uk

USA

www.coatsandclark.com

www.connectingthreads.com

www.hamelsfabrics.com

www.pinkchalkfabrics.com

Index

adhesives 9, 109
appliqué
  birthday party scenes 81
  bunting 81, 82, 83
  Christmas designs 90–1, 96–7
  fusible webbing 10, 32, 42
  hand 11
  letters 34
  machine 11
  name/date holders 82
  numbers 68, 117, 119
  wedding designs 56–7

baby projects 26–43, 110–13
backstitch 14
badges, birthday 68–9, 117
bags
baby gift bag 42–3
  drawstring 42–3, 50–1
  vintage posies 50–1
balloon designs 81–3
bar tacks 109
Bertie the Bear 84, 118
bibs, dribble 34–5, 113
binding 108
bird designs 42, 56–60, 114
birthday cakes
  appliqué 81, 119
  stuffed fabric 64–7
birthday projects 62–85, 116–20
blanket, first 32–3, 113
blanket stitch 15
bows 56–7, 96
bracelets, button 54–5
bridesmaids gifts 52–5, 224
brooches, button 52–3
bunting 22–5, 123
  appliqué 81, 82, 83
  baby 24, 123
  fabric requirements 24
  mini tree 92–5
  standard 24, 123
  vintage 24
  wedding 46–7, 115

buttons 46, 48, 60, 74, 76, 82–4, 90,
  96, 102
bracelets 54–5
brooches 52–3

candles, fabric 66
chain stitch 16
chick pennant 106–7, 124
Christmas projects 86–99, 121
Christmas tree mini bunting 92–5
coton à broder 9
cross stitch 20
crowns, fabric 76–7, 116
cupcake pennant 106–7, 125
cushion, ring 56–7, 114

date holders 82, 119
dogs, appliqué 81, 118
double-bound edges 108
dove designs 56–7, 114
drawstrings 42–3, 50–1
duck designs, embroidery 42

Easter designs 106–7, 124
embroidery 83–3
  for baby projects 32–42
  baby sampler 28–31
  birthday party stitchery 70–3
  Christmas designs 88–90, 92–5, 98
  lampshades 58–60, 88–90
  letters 36, 56, 58–60, 122
  for wedding projects 56, 58, 60
embroidery hoops 70–2
embroidery needles 9

fabrics 9
felt 9
French knot 19
friendship quilt 100–3
fusible webbing 10, 32, 42, 74, 76

gift bag, baby 42–3

Halloween designs 106–7, 125
hanging loops 85, 96
heart designs 74
  appliqué 32
  button brooches 52–3
  embroidery 58–60
hanging hearts 48–9, 114
herringbone stitch 18
hook-and-loop fasteners 66

key to the door pennant 106–7, 124

ladder stitch 109
lampshades
  Christmas 88–91, 121
  robin appliqué 90–1
  top table 58–61, 114
lazy daisy stitch 17
letters 34, 36, 56, 58–60, 122

maderia lana 9
Monogram alphabet 56, 58–60, 122

name holders 82, 119
needles, embroidery 9
numbers, appliqué 68, 117, 119

pennants 96–7, 104–7, 121, 124–5
pompoms 76, 96
posies, vintage 50–1
pumpkin pennant 106–7, 125

quilt sandwiches 109
quilts
  friendship/celebration 100–3
  wall hangings 82–3

rabbit, snuggle 36–9, 112
ribbons
  bows 56–7, 96
  for bunting 95
  drawstrings 42–3, 50–1
  hangers 48–9
  trims 68

ric-rac 48, 56–7, 64, 66, 74, 81–3, 96,
  102, 109
ring cushion 56–7, 114
robin designs
  appliqué lampshade 90–1
  Christmas pennant 96–7
  stuffed decorations 98–9, 121
running stitch 13

sampler, baby 28–31, 111
satin stitch 12
seven more sleeps hanging 78–85,
  118–19
shoes, first 40–1, 110
slip stitch 109
spray basting 109
stem stitch 21
stitchery, birthday party 70–3, 120
stitches
  directory 12–21
  starting/finishing 12
  utility 109
stranded cotton (floss) 9
sweet 16 pennant 106–7, 124

templates 110–25
threads 9
tiaras, fabric 74–5, 116
top table lampshades 58–61, 114
transferring designs 12

vintage
  bunting 24
  fabrics 9
  posies 50–1
  wedding designs 44–61

wall hanging, seven more sleeps
  78–85, 118–19
wedding projects 44–61, 114–15
whipped running stitch 13

DEDICATION

This book is dedicated to two very special people with whom I have had the pleasure of sharing many a good celebration ... Auntie Betty and Debbie. Thank you my darlings for your inspirations; you will be greatly missed.

A DAVID & CHARLES BOOK

© F&W Media International, Ltd 2013

David & Charles is an imprint of F&W Media International, Ltd
Brunel House, Forde Close, Newton Abbot, TQ12 4PU, UK

F&W Media International, Ltd is a subsidiary of F+W Media, Inc
10151 Carver Road, Suite #200, Blue Ash, OH 45242, USA

Text and Designs © Mandy Shaw 2013

Layout and Photography © F&W Media International, Ltd 2013

First published in the UK and USA in 2013

Mandy Shaw has asserted her right to be identified as author of this work in accordance with the Copyright, Designs and Patents Act, 1988.

A catalogue record for this book is available from the British Library.

ISBN-13: 978-1-4463-0264-4 paperback
ISBN-10: 1-4463-0264-4 paperback

Printed in China by RR Donnelley for:
F&W Media International, Ltd
Brunel House, Forde Close, Newton Abbot, TQ12 4PU, UK

10 9 8 7 6 5 4 3 2 1

Acquisitions Editor: Sarah Callard
Editor: Jeni Hennah
Project Editor: Cheryl Brown
Junior Art Editor: Anna Fazakerley
Photographer: Jack Kirby
Production Manager: Beverley Richardson

F+W Media publishes high quality books on a wide range of subjects.
For more great book ideas visit: www.stitchcraftcreate.co.uk